The Souls of Humanity

Past, Present and Future

Randi Green

The Souls of Humanity

Past, Present and Future

Contents

The True Soul Healer Education

The True Soul Healer Education is aimed at developing skilled healers to participate in the new paradigm of humanity. New understandings of what it means to be human are in progress all over the world.

Not as much on a political level, but from the roots of humanity, where the individual human feels the stir inside and the longing for something more, something better and something that will open up to the idea of humans being part of a universe, and parallel ones, with many different lifeforms.

The education has its foundation in this movement and then it goes beyond that. The goal is first and foremost to educate excellent healers, ready to work with the new models of what a human energy system is and the importance of understanding the stellar genetics, i.e. the foundation of consciousness and the stellar energy system.

The goal is also to instigate new beliefsystems, which will lead the student, and from them into the clients, to new insights and new evolutionary abilities.

Find out more on www.toveje.dk

This book is the history book for the first year of the True Soul Healer Education, but can be read as a book on its own. It is also useful if you want a template reading and you need to understand what the reading tells you of historical information, the genetics and so forth.

From the Beginning

We begin with a look into the first cosmos, the structures, inhabitants and connection to the Source Cycles, the oversoul cycles and the soul group cycles. It is important to understand what a soul is and how the evolutions unfold in the first cosmos. Then we investigate what led to the division of the soul races and the two universes that arose after this, i.e. the first disputes between the anti-elevation groups and the pro-elevation groups as well as the technologies and the result in the Internal Strife, which led to the division of the holographic metaverse (the HM), giving grounds for the less-progressive universe (the LPU). We look into the soul races that departed and what they faced as settlers in a new type of universe.

We will look into the technologies they took with them and their later inventions leading to more problems for the departed soul races. We look at the participation and evolutions of the LPU and the new divisions among the departed soul races. Which role does the technologically enhanced genetics (the TEGs) play and how do they affect the LPU evolutions? What obstacles do the races of the LPU face as a part of this system cut off from holographic universe? How have they solved this?

From here we move on into the historical details of the LPU, the collaborations, the timeline event and the rise of the ancient stellar races.

Then the regression fields and their races are addressed. It is from here the Reptilian Riots arose and we need to look into the background of the regressive races and what led to the takeover of our planet. What were the reasons for the Reptilian Riots? How did it affect the lower levels of the less-progressive universe? And when did the dark ones get into power of our reality field, the technologies in humans etc?

Finally the technologies in humans are looked into and the stellar factions behind. The future of the astral barrier is also looked into. The rescue missions into the LPU and why they were instigated are addressed as well.

The Source Cycles

When we attempt to understand how everything came to be, we lack words. It is quite impossible to grasp the origin of our being and what is behind all that exists. However since the mind needs a beginning to operate with, I will give an analogy for the purpose. It is nothing more than an image and not *the truth*. The truth about what is behind all that exist is non-comprehensible since it exists outside manifestation and the mind can only grasp things that are manifested. What we can grasp is the first nature of manifestation which is Source. And again a redefinition is in place since the true Source is not one type of origin, but *one out of many*. The diverse versions of Source are called Source Cycles and each cycle express an idea of manifestation as energy, consciousness or something entirely else we cannot understand so far. Source Cycles manifest from *the Infinity* and the Infinity is totally out of our reach to define. Hence the first manifestation is the Source Cycles.

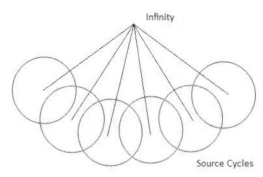

Infinity

Source Cycles

The Source Cycles unfold different ideas from which whole universes and entities take form. The succession of ideas varies according to the progression of the ideas, which grow and evolve into something else. *The ideas of manifestation are not determined by a choice or some sort of will.* The concept of a great something holding a will with its creation, is a projection of mind wanting to give features to the Source Cycles. For that reason, when it is understood that Source is part of various forms of expressions and only represent *one version of a Source Cycle*, it becomes clearer that any form of projection with the aim to give rise to some sort of will or determination of what is to unfold, arises from the immature state of mind, needing some variety of a creator to take responsibility for the well-being of us.

The cosmological advanced mind understands that Source Cycles are determined by laws and effects that arise out of succession and that the only determining principle there is, is the individual itself. The statement "God is in you" is to be taken literally since we are the creators and not the creation of a god. We are the extension of *the core consciousness principles* governing a universe and it is up to us to create with these principles, not to function as an extension of a higher will we are part of.[1] Succession or progression is continuously and do as such not begin because its point of origin is in *the Infinity*. From Infinity all things arise out of no-where and they will continue to exist as long as Infinity is there, which is forever. Hence there is no beginning and no end given the fact that the Source Cycles pull their origin from the Infinity, i.e. the forever and ever state of presence.

Consequently any speculation of what began the whole thing is fruitless and we only get to some level of understanding, when we accept the non-sentient foundation of our origin found in progression and continuously evolution of ideas that change according to the forever and ever infusion of the Infinity.

---

[1] The goal is to regain the sovereignty of our core consciousness and not give it away to something outside of us. We are the sole creators, the god, and the ones that hold the responsibility of this and any creation; not a creator because there is no creator.

The Oversoul Cycles

To get closer to the understanding of our origin, the level after the Source Cycles has to be understood as well. Here we get the first level that unfolds our present level of progression.

Since the Source Cycle, we are part of, is presently unfolding *the idea of consciousness*, whereas the previous Source Cycle unfolded *the idea of energy*, I will return to the understanding of this later on when a context is offered to understand it, it will suffice to say here that the oversoul cycles are the first manifest expression of a Source Cycle.

A Source Cycle is an idea that emanates from the Infinity and only from the level of the oversouls does the process of manifestation turn into something we can comprehend. Everything before that is only grasped from the level of intuition.

The Progressive OverSoul Cycles that Unfold from One Source Cycle

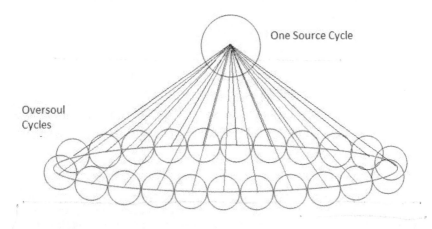

The oversoul cycles are the first level where some notion of existence comes into play. The oversoul cycles qualify as the highest level of our reality unfolding the idea of consciousness into something that is able to unfold as existence, holding of type of will and determination, and not as ideas floating around being fueled by the Infinity.

Nevertheless the oversoul cycles unfold according to the pull of progression, succession, laws and repeated powers. The oversoul cycles are the closest we get to something holding the principal notion of all the lower cycles that emanate from the oversoul cycles.

The oversoul cycles are to be understood *as principles*. Principles hold a distinguishable character of something that is different from the other principles and express a set of dynamics that unfold the ideas of manifestation. Therefore each of the oversoul cycles hold a set of principles that unfold into minor units with the purpose of making these units unfold the principles into existence. Each oversoul cycle is determined by these principles and they are to unfold all of the possibilities and probabilities of the principles into universes holding the idea of the Source Cycle and the progression level that is in play from the Infinity.

As it is seen on the illustration of the Source Cycles, the cycles overlap. One Source Cycle merges into a new *when the principles from the oversoul cycles progress and develop into a new oversoul cycle.* Hence the Source Cycle and the oversoul cycles are interdependent. The idea unfolding in a Source Cycle cannot be expressed unless the principles of the oversoul cycles are unfolded into existence. The oversoul cycles are thus the first level of existence, which is expressed as principles. The principles of existence have been called many things in the secret

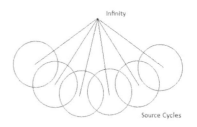

Infinity

Source Cycles

teachings: the firstborn sons of God, the inarticulate pure ones, the ones holding the secrets of all that exist etc. As mentioned each oversoul cycle holds several principles expressing the idea of the Source Cycle they manifest into being-ness.

The principles are the catalyst of the possibilities and probabilities the idea of consciousness (or energy or something entirely else) is able to unfold and they form the next level of existence, which is called the soul groups.

Soul Group Cycles

Everything is consciousness in *the unified consciousness field*. That is a statement that needs some serious consideration and meditation. Actually this is impossible to grasp until you are in contact with your soul, because does the soul has a size, a shape or form? Does it hold individuality or is it just a tiny blimp floating around in the ocean of pure light, pure consciousness and pure thought?

Well, describing something that exists outside our present reality field is hard enough to grasp; that is in another dimension, but to grasp something that holds no dimension, form or shape is even more difficult because the closest we get is to see the soul as *the sensation of principles*. For the sake of the understanding I wish to share with you, I will attempt to describe the soul to the best of my ability and the unified consciousness field it stem from.

The unified consciousness field is an extension of the oversoul cycles, into which the soul groups manifest. A unified field is a field of consciousness gathered into a huge "something" which the Greeks called Cosmos. In a cosmos something exists as something; a sort of space into which something exists or a collaboration of existence that is both individual and collective. When the unified consciousness field acts as a collective the units in it are non-distinctive from the whole; everything is a unified field of existence. When the whole divides into units, the whole becomes a cosmos or a place, where the units can unfold their existence as individuals. The unified consciousness field holds both levels of existence. Thus being means to exist. However it takes more to understand the soul groups, which turn into the soul races, when they unfold into form in the holographic metaverse. In

17

the unified consciousness field the soul groups exist as *collectives of consciousness units*.

The highest division of the oversoul cycles, i.e. the principles of creation, is found in the consciousness units when they enter the holographic metaverse through *the soul gates* and are turned into what we perceive as souls. The consciousness units hold all of the properties of the idea of their Source Cycle as well as the principles that are expressed in the oversoul cycles.

Soul gates are tunnels between the holographic metaverse and the unified consciousness field, in which the consciousness units exist as collectives. A soul gate is not placed in time or space, but is called the "eye of the needle" because only the consciousness units are tiny enough to enter the eye and return to the unified consciousness field.

To become that small, the consciousness units have to have transformed all holographic material to be able to enter *the eye of its own existence*. Hence only the consciousness units know when the time is up to let go of the holographic metaverse and return to the pool of unity and pure existence in the unified consciousness field or if the job is well done, to continue into the next Source Cycle. The time for return cannot be taught, learned or explained.

When the consciousness units are ready, they climb towards the true light[2] by having transformed all they have been, will be and could become because they are done with the evolutionary cycles, they had been pulled into. Being done does not mean to hold any emotional connotation to it, as in "I long for home" or "I am tired and want the present existence to end". These statements express emotions from the ego and have nothing to do with the consciousness units. The consciousness units have no sense of self since they are an expression

---

[2] I am not talking about the tunnel of light we hear of in near death experiences. These tunnels are artificial and lead to the false "soul groups" of the astral plane, which is a psychological level of existence inside the astral barrier.

of principles, hence they cannot say "I feel or think". These sensations are properties of the ego. The ego is the "I". No, the consciousness units have no shape or form, and yet they can take on a form. They can grow from being nothing to become something. Why do they do this? Not because of an inner impulse to become but as a response from the evolutionary cycles they are to become part of. When the soul groups, the consciousness units are an integral part of, get ready to change into *the seven evolutionary cycles*, the soul groups divide and change according to the pull of the evolutionary cycles and first then do the soul groups turn into consciousness units.

Again the division of a Source Cycle into oversouls and soul groups has nothing to do with an inner impulse stemming from any notion of I, but is a response of the previous cycle that came before the present one. When one cycle is done, the next is activated. The cycles are eternal and they did not as such begin and they will never end. They unfold from lesser to more, from more to lesser and from lesser to more again developing all thinkable evolutionary cycles of higher and smaller divisions. Thus the consciousness units enter the holographic metaverse due to the pull of the evolutionary cycles, holding a specific set of possibilities and probabilities to unfold. These are determined by the previous evolutionary cycles and their soul groups and so forth back up to the Source Cycle that is in play. And thus the consciousness units return to the unified consciousness field, or the soul group, when they have unfolded and transformed all of the potentials they got from the soul groups and their cycles. Only then will the consciousness units return through the eye of the needle.

All entering into the holographic metaverse is an automatic pull instigated by the higher and lower cycles through the soul gates and the returning back is automatic as well when the "job" is done. Only when the consciousness units have unfolded all of the possibilities and probabilities, outliving all of principles into being able to interact directly with the consciousness units by the transformation of the intermediary means of genetics, energy systems, organic forms and holographic resonance fields, are the consciousness units able to climb the "mountain of God" and enter the eye or gate at the top.

A *soul group*, i.e. collective of consciousness units, has its own duration of possibilities and probabilities to unfold and transform. Thus a soul group is in play, in the holographic metaverse, until all of these possibilities and probabilities are mastered to their fullest and then transformed. Then a soul group is done and all of the remaining units are "lifted" into the next soul group level.

Naturally some of the consciousness units progress faster than others and some soul groups do not make it to the cut, compared to the other soul groups before the next cycle is instigated from the soul groups having made the cut and thus are pulled to the next level of the evolutionary cycles. When a soul group does not make it, the consciousness units in that soul group are put on hold, or go into *pralaya* as the Hindus called it.

Pralaya means that a soul group is unable to follow the pull of the next cycle and is therefore left behind. The consciousness units are pulled back into their soul groups from the cycle that goes out of existence, but the group does not unfold into the next evolutionary cycle. The soul group has to wait for a new evolutionary cycle that matches the possibilities and probabilities that this soul group is able to unfold in the holographic metaverse. Sometimes a soul group has to sit-over for one or two whole soul group cycles before a level of the holographic metaverse match the possibilities and probabilities of the sit-over soul group. Then the group with its consciousness units is pulled back into play and gets a new chance of unfolding all of the possibilities and probabilities with the goal of making it to the next evolutionary cycle. With this in mind, it is easy to understand why the understanding of individual sovereignty of being the sole creator, is important to comprehend and not the idea of a god that takes care of everything. If we await some sort of god to pull us to the next level, we are to wait forever, since the pull comes from our progression and not instigated by divine intervention. To exist, means to do the best that is possible to be able to take part of the pull of the cycles.

The Holographic Metaverse

Now where does the holographic metaverse stem from? The easy answer is that it is the result of earlier oversoul and soul group cycles. But this does not really explain the notion of the division of energy and consciousness. However if it is understood that it has not been until the present Source Cycle that the oversoul cycles with their soul groups were able to unfold consciousness and that they before this unfolded energy, i.e. vibration and radiation, it is easier to understand that the vibration and radiation the present soul groups are to merge and transform by the use of consciousness, are the result of a prior Source Cycle where the principles were expressed as vibration and radiation. In this Source Cycle the idea is to express consciousness, and by this transform the prior idea. In the next Source Cycle the idea will be something else, determined by the automatic cycles of lesser and more.

The soul groups created the holographic metaverse in the previous evolutionary cycles where the progression units, i.e. the soul groups existed as vibration and radiation in a unified field of energy. This field had soul gates linked to a rough version of a metaverse, where the energy units would manifest as vibration and radiation with the purpose of developing the rough metaverse into finer definitions of vibration and radiation. The holographic metaverse was the result of their effort and it holds all what the energy units build in through the progression processes of the oversoul groups, the soul groups and the energy units that manifested the possibilities and probabilities of that Source Cycle into existence of vibration and radiation (energy).

Everything in the Holographic Metaverse is Light Coding
The holographic metaverse entirely consists of vibration and radiation expressed through units called light coding. If the Source Cycle and the oversoul cycles were still expressing vibration and radiation as the main idea with its principles, we would be surrounded by energy and there would be no distinction between *the previous unified energy field* and the holographic metaverse.

However the Source Cycle has changed and is now consciousness, making the goal in this cycle to master the energies through the new existence, i.e. the expression of the principles as consciousness. The vibration and radiation principles have moved from being the prime of the previous cycle into becoming the foundation of this cycle, i.e. light coding and how it that?

Whereas energy is to be seen as the foundation of a cosmos, consciousness holds the features of existence. In the previous Source Cycle energy was all that existed. The energy took form as vibration and radiation and existed as the possibilities and probabilities the vibration and radiation held. So what exists and what does not, is hidden in what the Source Cycles express as existence. Given that the Source Cycle has changed and is expressing the idea of consciousness, only units made of consciousness is able to be one with the oversouls.

The energy units that created the holographic metaverse have retracted to their oversoul cycles or have gone into pralaya, however their playground remains. Whereas the return of the units in this soul group cycle is determined by the level of transformation, the previous cycle was determined by the level of refinement of the vibration and radiation energies, denoting a sort of classification of energies into the lowest and highest possible refinement. The correct level gave

22

access to the withdrawal through the soul gates. The ones that retracted and made the cut have turned into consciousness units in this cycle. Consciousness is in that sense a highly refined form of merged vibration and radiation. By this the consciousness units are returning to the holographic metaverse, they built when they existed as energy units. Thus the energies creating the holographic metaverse are the remnants of the units as they existed in the previous oversoul cycle. The soul groups are returning to the holographic metaverse to develop their former manifestation into realigning with the existence of this Source Cycle.

Some refer to the holographic metaverse as the divine mother, or the type of matter into which the present oversoul and soul groups of consciousness can take form. The holographic metaverse is here seen as the womb where consciousness is able to be seeded and transform the energies into the present existence, unfolding the merging of the two. The merging becomes the child of the previous Source Cycle and its oversouls (the mother) and the present Source Cycles and its oversouls (the father). This symbolism is seen all over in mythology and stem from the intuitive understanding that all is the same, but in different states; as the mother, the father and the child. Now; to fully understanding the mother energy, or the energies from the previous Source Cycle surrounding us and building our present forms, worlds, reality fields and galaxies, we have to understand the units of energy, vibration and radiation. These are different states of light coding.

Light coding is the units that build the forms, worlds, reality fields and universes of the present evolutionary cycles. Light coding is the "language to understand the former version of existence". When we master the light coding we are able to create using the energies of the previous units of existence and we are in this reconnecting to a former version of ourselves. It is important to remember this and not make a distinction of vibration and radiation as being archaic or bad, but as a different state of units, which in essence are us. The light coding is the principles of existence in an older form and should be revered as such.

Light coding has different states: as energy which is the unity and as vibration and radiation, which is energy divided into its subforms.

Vibration has the feature of movement and dynamics whereas *radiation* has the feature of emission and form-building. Light coding can be set up to generate vibration or radiation all depending on the type of energy that is utilized. When I here say energy, I mean units from the previous soul group cycle. Energy units do not have a form or shape, but are the state of possibilities and probabilities of the expression of the previous principles.

Consequently the possibilities and probabilities can be expressed as vibration, holding a specific set of light coding or as radiation, holding another type of light coding. Consciousness units of this cycle have to reach a high degree of knowledge before they can master the energies of the previous cycle since they are now unfolded through a new set of principles of existence and the old set is forgotten, so to speak. The work with the light coding is performed by the use of form and the changing of these. The forms are built of radiation and the changes are vibration in essence, generating what we understand as holographic resonance fields and systems.

Manifestation of Souls

Manifestation happens when the consciousness units are integrated into energy. Not until the consciousness units enter the holographic metaverse do they become manifest and get a sense of existence as an entity, because the consciousness units are nothing and everything in the unified consciousness field. Light coding is gathered when the consciousness units enter through the soul gates into the holographic metaverse. The radiation generates the blueprint of form to the units and the vibration attracts identical energies from the surrounding holographic resonance field. Only when a form, through light coding as radiation, is created can the light coding as vibration be attracted to manifest a holographic form. In the holographic metaverse the consciousness units enter into the work place of the previous cycle. As mentioned, this happens automatically and the consciousness units do not choose to come into manifestation; it happens when the time is ripe and the cycle is up. The consciousness units (also called light units) fuse with the light coding (also called holographic units) as sperm does with an egg and from the merging of the light coding and the consciousness units, a sphere or an orb is created.

This is the best image I can give you, however it is still an image and therefore not what really happens, given that the light coding and consciousness units do not have a perimeter, which a sphere or orb has per definition. The orb is what we call a *soul*.

After the fusion with light coding the consciousness units begin to grow inside the orb (the soul) and generate numerous new units called soul genetics, holding the principles that were stored in the consciousness units to begin with, albeit in the genetics the principles get divided into even smaller units. The principles unfolded into the genetics then become the possibilities and probabilities the fused light coding and light units are able to manifest and transform.

The orb with the soul genetics is then drawn to the holographic resonance field[3] that fits the soul genetics in the orb by identical radiation and vibration levels. In the holographic resonance field (the HRF) the soul genetics inside the orb, attracts new holographic coding from the holographic resonance field and a suitable form for the evolutionary sequence is generated. Then life as we know it begins to unfold, holding a soul and a form. These are the soul races.

---

[3] Read more about the HRFs under the General Level.

Given that the consciousness units of all of the soul groups, which are ready to do so, enter the holographic metaverse simultaneously, all life in the metaverse unfolds synchronistically.

When an evolutionary cycle begins in the holographic metaverse there is no real beginning or ending; there are phases of evolution that could be seen as "then there was nothing and then there was all". The soul races and their holographic resonance fields inside the holographic metaverse thus arise "over night" on their own and not by the hands of any creator.

The oversoul cycles determine what unfolds in the holographic metaverse and the moment the soul groups as collectives of consciousness units enter through the soul gates, realities arise and the soul races flourishes instantly.

The Seven Evolutionary Cycles

The ideas spring forth from the Infinity as Source Cycles. From the Source Cycles the principles emanate as oversoul cycles and from here collectives of consciousness units establish the soul group cycles.

Soul group cycles are fields of progression where the idea and its principles can unfold all of the levels consciousness is able to hold as potentials and possibilities. The unified consciousness field and its units generate the blueprint for as many realities as possible, based upon the idea and its principles, i.e. the laws of progression, existence and manifestation.

First when we reach the evolutionary cycles, do we begin to have holographic resonance fields were entities unfold their evolutionary progress as the transition from one Source Cycle, via the principles in the oversoul cycles, to another Source Cycle, bridging or merging the two Source Cycles into one main cycle. In this main cycle the principles (oversoul cycles) of the previous cycles meet the principles of the present cycle and merges fully into the new Source Cycle. Into this conglomerate of merging principles, holographic resonance fields are unfolded holding even smaller units. The transitions of the Source Cycles are expressed into seven evolutionary cycles where the units of energy or consciousness can undergo the evolution from being an idea and its principles into becoming units of existence manifested as metaverse awareness, self-awareness and perception of awareness.

First Evolutionary Cycle (the dot)
The first evolutionary cycle manifested the cores of all holographic resonance fields (the HRFs). A HRF is created, in lack of a better word,

when the oversoul cycles extend and divide into fields, each having a distinct set of principles. The first level was the unified consciousness field generating the soul groups, from where the consciousness units entered the holographic metaverse, i.e. the overall pool of energy from the previous Source Cycle. However this is only one of the emanations the oversoul cycles instigated. Given that the oversoul cycles unfolded the holographic metaverse in the previous Source Cycle, the transitions from one Source Cycle and into the new, keep the energy fields of the previous oversoul cycles intact until the idea of energy in the previous Source is fully outlived and transformed, leaving only the new Source Cycle to be the one main cycle.

The oversoul cycle of this Source Cycle seeded several huge light units[4] into the holographic metaverse, generated in the previous Source Cycle, and brought it back to life and by this made it ready to receive the consciousness units in a later evolutionary cycle. The huge light units turned into the cores of dissimilar holographic resonance fields, each with their own set of light coding. The cores held, and hold, the principles to be unfolded into the holographic resonance fields with the goal of transforming them, laying the foundation for all later expressions of existence to pick up on.

The circumference of a core and its holographic resonance fields are the foundation of a certain level of existence. The foundation of the new levels of existence, with the holographic resonance fields and core principles, held and hold a unique set of principles to be unfolded on that level and manifested into the various forms of light coding each holographic resonance fields hold.

For many the core principles is perceived as the Source of all there is, since it holds the will behind that level of existence, i.e. the laws of that level and the goal with it.

---

[4] Light units hold the consciousness of these cycles, whereas light coding is made out of the energies of the previous oversoul cycles.

Second Evolutionary Cycle (the vertical line)

From the seeding of the core principles into the surrounding fields of light coding a transition took place, the holographic metaverse and energies from the previous Source Cycle transformed into a new version of light coding fields, holding a specific amount of the core principles all depending on the level of existence in that HRF. The lower leveled HRFs hold lesser amounts of core principles since they are placed in the outer rings of the circumference and thus far away from the core principles, and the higher leveled HRFs hold larger amounts of core principles, because they are closer to the core. The HRFs can thus hold more or less amounts of core principles. The division of the HRFs, being either close or far away from the core, sets the playing ground for the lifeforms that later on will unfold there.

Third Evolutionary Cycle (the triangle)

After the HM had been reconstructed into the new settings, a new division took place, dividing the HRFs into spatial fields. The further out we get from the core principles, the less core consciousness is embedded in that holographic resonance fields. But the HRFs are not enough on their own to unfold lifeforms; they are to be seen as fields of possibilities and probabilities.

The spatial fields unfold from the HFRs and the cores, into spaces having gridworks. The spaces of a HRF can be understood by looking into the spatial features a dimensional reality field in our universe holds; e.g. a 3rd dimensional reality field has three levels of perception: height, depth and breadth. The 3rd dimensional reality fields are mostly based upon particles, but not as atomic forces, more like quantum sub-atomic particles. A 4th dimensional reality field holds height, depth, breadth and then there is the last dimension which extends into the other three, making the space dynamic and interactive. The 4th dimensional field[5] consists of particles and waves, where the features of reality respond differently.

A 5th dimensional reality field holds the features of the other two dimensions, although there are no particles; the energy is expressing the spatial features as height, depth, breadth, but these are made of waves instead.

Holographic gridworks based upon quantum flux fields hold the principles of the spatial field they exist in as probabilities (the light coding) with a dormant core of possibilities (the light units in the core).

Holographic gridworks based upon quantum waves consist of activated consciousness, i.e. activated possibilities merged with light coding, which makes the gridworks build of waves unfold properties we can only dream of. Here consciousness and light coding interact directly with each other.

Fourth Evolutionary Cycle (the quadrant)

From the spatial features the holographic resonance fields unfolded yet a division where new units were expressed from the spatial fields. The new units were individual forms, arising from the holographic resonance field as conglomerates of light coding and light units. The forms were generated to unfold the features of the gridwork energies and as a symbol the forms can be viewed as quadrants or squares of energy. The consciousness units as individuals were then ready to be pulled into the holographic metaverse.

The first lifeforms of the soul races were as forms on all four legs evolving the soul genetics; i.e. the light units giving life to a form. They unfolded the insectoid, avian, reptoid and mammal genetics in the fourth evolutionary cycle. The four-legged form is often referred

_____

[5] Look up on the internet who four dimensional geometry looks like.

to as the animal phase of human evolution, albeit in this context is not animals as we see them today on our planet, but highly intelligent lifeforms with a soul orb, being forced to walk on all four legs due to the undeveloped spatial fields holding a comprised type of energies.

The comprised energies have nothing to do with densities of the LPU, but were the result of the undeveloped holographic settings having little activated core principles.

Although some of the HRFs had higher amounts of core principles, the lifeforms had to activate and evolve it from the depths of the fields, they unfolded from. In the outskirts of the HRFs, in the lower leveled HRFs, there were no lifeforms unfolded because the lowest areas were unfit for any forms of life and only held holographic energy. Thus the first lifeforms spread out in the level, which is called the holographic resonance field three (HRF3) of the holographic metaverse.

The undeveloped light coding was heavier and less flexible, which is why the first lifeforms were forced to walk on all four. The different gridworks were there, but they only held this early version of the light coding with a dormant core of the possibilities of consciousness. As the lifeforms developed the energies of the fourth evolutionary cycle, the core principles of the HRFs expanded the light units from within, transforming the light coding of the forms and fields.

This gave room for a more upright position in the next version of lifeforms. The fourth evolutionary cycle was all about evolving the spatial fields from the undeveloped type of light coding into a less comprised form.

The soul races of the fourth evolutionary cycle had no individual personality as such but were directly linked up to their soul groups outside the holographic metaverse to ensure that they would not get "lost" in the extremely complex forms of light coding.

Fifth Evolutionary Cycle (the pentagram)

After having taking a full cycle as four-legged forms, the soul races entered the fifth evolutionary system as two-legged humanoid forms.

A humanoid form of the fifth evolutionary cycle had the features and traits of the forms of the fourth evolutionary cycle, but due to the less comprised light coding, the forms now took on the pentagram shape having a head, a torso, two legs and two arms in an upright position. The lesser comprised light coding, i.e. light coding with a higher level of activated core principles, gave room to a variety of finer energies were the core principles of the HRFs were able to permeate the humanoid body as light units.

The larger amount of activated light units in the humanoid form generated a copy of the core principles into the individual humanoid although not identical since there are many possibilities of what the core principles can unfold. The copy of the core principles inside the humanoid form is called *the core consciousness*.

Since the core consciousness were held in an container of light coding, repeating the forever ongoing process of transforming the light coding from within by activating the light units in them and develop all of the light coding into merged light coding and light units, the copy of the core principles gave the ability to process light coding into a state of perception that could be seen as something dissimilar from the rest of the groups of humanoid. The individual personality of the humanoids arose by this dynamic, differing according to the evolved state of the light units hidden inside the light coding of the form as well as the amount of activated core principles in the HRF, expressed as core consciousness in the humanoid.

The goal of the fifth evolutionary cycle is therefore, we are still in it, to activate the core consciousness reflecting and expressing the core principles into the individual form. When the core principles are unfolded as light units inside the light coding, it transforms them into a merged light coding-light unit type of consciousness infused energy, making the humanoid form change into a totally new type of entity. Again, we are presently taking part of the fifth evolutionary cycle.

Sixth Evolutionary Cycle (the hexagram)

From the humanoid pentagram, the next evolutionary cycle unfolds when the soul races enter the metaverse as true humans with the goal of evolving the core consciousness directly into the form holding merged light coding with an activated light unit type of energy (I do not know what to call it, since it does not exist yet). The HRFs of the sixth cycle will be even less comprised and the energy systems, or blueprint for the lifeforms, will be unfolded as spheres with a type of energy-consciousness that is incomprehensible to us. The core consciousness will emit flows of transformed vibration as well as generating a field of radiation merged with consciousness. The flows and the high level of active light units generate the sphere shape. How the form will be, is up to the entities to choose.

The sixth evolutionary cycle true human will be directly connected to the core principles, now fully expressed into the HRFs, linking all lifeforms directly to the core of the holographic resonance fields and the rest of the holographic metaverse unfolding the core principles into large manifestations of unity and individuality. There will be no separation of the core principles of the HRFs and the core consciousness of the individual entity, which means that all lifeforms will synchronistically activate the HRFs, and transform them into the same type of fusion of light coding with a core of activated light units. The transformation of the previous oversoul manifestation will be over when the individual lifeforms, the HRFs and the overall metaverse transform into the new type of energy-consciousness and "burn up" all of the divisions into one whole, all expressing the core principles as a unity.

Seventh Evolutionary Cycle (the circle with the dot in the middle)
The seventh evolutionary cycle is a short one, since in this cycle all of the units that did not make it in the previous six cycles are separated and go into pralaya and the rest retract to the oversoul level, getting ready to begin a new oversoul cycle.

The Soul Races of the Fourth and Fifth Evolutionary Cycles
The soul races have existed in the holographic metaverse for eons in these two cycles with the aim to evolve and manifest the principles of the oversoul cycles. The soul races are expressed as five different types of soul genetics; i.e. light coding with a core of light units from the unified consciousness field. Four versions of the genetics evolved in the fourth evolutionary cycle, i.e. the insectoid, avian, reptoid and mammal. The fifth type of soul genetics, the true human, is yet to be developed but some hold the pre-stages of it.

The soul races hold the different types of genetics with various intensity; being the amount of light coding having unfolded the core consciousness, and they are all in the progression of evolving the animal genetics of the fourth evolutionary cycle into the standards of the present fifth cycle. Thus in this present fifth cycle the soul races are to develop the animal genetics, i.e. the insectoid, avian, reptoid and mammal genetics into combinations, which make them able to hold higher levels of light units.

The progression goal of the fifth cycle is to evolve the potentials of the true human genetic level (the fifth type of genetics) enabling the soul races to enter the sixth evolutionary cycle and later into the seventh cycle, where this oversoul cycles ends.

The Less-Progressive Universe

Before we move into the division of the fifth evolutionary cycle, it might be in order to take a look into the less-progressive universe, we are part of, so that the questions related to this is addressed and by this make more room for the history that unfolded before the less-progressive universe came into existence. Contrary to the holographic metaverse were everything is fueled and ruled by the oversoul principles, the less-progressive universe is fueled by an artificial core, called the central sun, which was created to keep the fields of the less-progressive universe energetically stable. The LPRF5[6] creators of the central sun were the deflectors from the soul races that chose to go on their own and generate a secondary holographic universe, I have named the less-progressive universe. In the less-progressive universe everything is created and controlled by LPRF5 races, which originated as part of the metaverse soul races. Nothing in the less-progressive universe unfolds as an impulse from the principles, given that the oversoul cycles have little connection to the less-progressive universe.

LPU Genetics and Energy Systems
It is achievable to engineer a holographic form holding no or less amounts of soul genetics in the less-progressive universe, since light coding holds the pre-stages of consciousness. Due to the artificial core of the less-progressive universe, new holographic solutions were needed to be able to exist in this universe and the invention of a template with genetics and the extension of these into an energy

---

[6] Less-progressive reality field five races.

system was the solution. Nonetheless this type of form often runs on technologically enhanced genetics (Tegs) and they cannot progress or evolve into something higher. The form holds a personality and mind, but it cannot exceed the potentials of the artificial genetics it holds, unless the TEGs are modified or new TEGs are installed.

The technological enhanced genetics come in different versions and shapes; some of them hold bits of soul genetics and others are fully artificial. The TEGs break down and dissolve over time.

They are also prone to unfold what is called the infection. The infection is when a TEG breaks totally down and then turns dark. An infected TEG is called technological enhanced *infected* genetics or TEIGs. Being dark means to do all that is harmful and against every law of any evolutionary cycle. If a being holding TEGs turn dark, he or she has no control over the form s/he is in. S/he is fully controlled by the TEIGs and nothing can turn a being in a fully infected state back to become "light", i.e. being able to progress according to the plan of the cycles. A fully infected TEGs energy system that holds a dissolving template is called a dark one. The dark ones dissolve when the integrated genetics in the energy system dissolve into dust. Therefore the dark ones[7] have survived by becoming parasites sucking the genetics out of other stellar humanoids. We will return to the dark ones later on.

The soul genetics, TEGs or LPU genetics in the template are called template genetics. Genetics from the template that are integrated into the vortexes of the energy system are called *integrated genetics* and the set of light coding unfolding an organic or dimensional body is called *biological genetics*, or bio-genetics for short.

---

[7] The dark ones are also called the dark masters. The dark ones exist predominantly in the 4th, the 5th and the 7th dimension since the 6th dimensional races have solved the problem of the infection by going crystalline using the silicate type of matter and the 8-12 stranded template. These strands are a new version of TEGs.

The Division of the Fifth Evolutionary Cycle

Time is dynamic and changes with the genetics viewing the timelines. Thus since the light unit ratio of the timelines[8] of our reality field is changing, as more humans activate their integrated genetics, the result is that the energetic set up in the gridworks of the DE1D3[9] is speeding up. When and if the timelines reach a certain ratio, the gridwork they are embedded into will attempt to re-attach to the still functioning stargates (dimensional bridges) and by this bridge to the progressive dynamics of the higher levels of the LPU. If this happens time will disappear entirely.

Time is dynamic and changes with the flows of energy that run in the gridworks of a reality field. When our DE1D3 is restored back into its original DE1D3 holographic settings, there will be no past or future, only dissimilar features of the reality fields surrounding us. *Three factors contribute to our perception of history:*

1. The fact that a timeline event generated the explosion-split-resetting dynamics that expanded as a tidal wave from a LPRF3 reality field. As a result the reality fields of the LPRF3 and the LPRF2 were rearranged. The quantum flux fields were distorted and solidified, creating a sort of organic holographic energy.

2. The solidification atrophied many of the LPRF3 and LPRF2 areas and changed their reality fields and lifeforms into a type

---

[8] One reality field holds many subrealities called timelines. A timeline sets the perception field of the embodied genetics. Therefore within one reality field of a density, there can be multiple reality fields holding multiple timelines and hence multiple outcome of existence. Perception and existence are interconnected.

[9] DE1D3: Density one, 3rd dimension.

of matter based upon light coding features that differed from the original settings of less-progressive universe. These were called densities and dimensions.

3. The new lifeforms developed into *the ancient stellar races* having an organic form and a new type of bio-genetics.

4. In terms of archeological findings of bones and fossils etc. many of the remnants are not of old age but a result of the atrophying process that took place after the timeline event.

5. That our perception of time and thus of history have been altered via the reversed light coding of an enclosure, creating an *inner barrier of perception* between our reality field and the adjacent DE1D3 fields, preventing other stellar races from getting in contact with us telepathically. The enclosure has produced a layer between the DE1D3 energy system and the rest of the DE1D3 reality fields, as well as unfolded an entire new reality of astral energies, i.e. the astral plane, housing various astral entities.

The division of the fifth evolutionary cycle that led into two dissimilar holographic universes, of which one is the holographic metaverse with its huge holographic resonance fields generated by the original soul races, and the other turned into the less-progressive universe housing the less-progressive races, is a complicated matter and naturally we cannot go into all of the details. We are forced to only focus on the broad strokes in the periods where major shifts occurred. Most details of the various reality fields and their multiple timelines are left out and as the individual memories surface in the minds of present day humans, the left out details will be reinstated into the history of the fifth cycle. Nevertheless everything has to start somewhere and the division of the fifth evolutionary cycle is a good place to begin.

The Internal Strife
The internal strife separated the holographic metaverse (the HM) into two different factions of the soul races; i.e. the original soul races and the less-progressive races.

The internal strife began in the HRF5 meta-councils of the upper leveled soul races of the higher developed humanoids, representing the soul genetics that had reached the highest potentials of their holographic resonance field (the HRFs), and thus had the highest level of interconnection to the core principles. These upper leveled HRF soul races were the leaders of the meta-councils and from here all decisions of evolution in the lower leveled HRFs, as well as among the soul races, took place there.[10]

The disputes were about what to do with certain factions of soul races inside the lower leveled HRFs that were not able to keep up with the progression dynamics of their reality field and thus were in the risk zone of being pulled untimely into pralaya, which would harm the other lower leveled HRFs and their soul races. One faction of the meta-councils advocated for the need to put a hold to *the third elevation cycle,* which would lift the lower leveled soul races to the next HRF to continue their evolution there.[11] The soul races, which were not being able to meet the requirements of the next HRF, i.e. could not match the new light coding-light unit ratio, would be pulled into pralaya unless something was done. A faction of the HRF5 meta-councils was more into the idea of continuing the natural progression dynamics and then re-balancing the remaining soul races afterwards

---

[10] Soul races of the metaverse unfold in forms that are very similar to the ones we find inside the less-progressive universe, since the form used here stem from the holographic metaverse. The main difference between the less-progressive universe and the metaverse is not in the forms or reality fields, but in the progression dynamics that run them.

[11] The elevation cycles are seven minor cycles within the major seven evolutionary cycles, lifting the soul races from the lower dimensions to the higher.

and a minor faction of concerned citizens of the HRF3 and HRF4 came up with the idea of inventing technologies that could generate an accelerated activation of the light units dormant inside the light coding and by that method meet the required ratio. Since excessively many of the HRF2 soul races had not reached the required ratio to be able to elevate, the accelerated transformation technologies were chosen as the solution.

As a consequence of this decision lots of experiments were done to enhance the genetics to enable the lower leveled races to follow the third elevation cycle. However they failed and the outcome was a great political conflict based upon the assisting HRF3 and HRF4 races, along with the HRF2 races, wanting to hold back the uplifting against the ones that supported leaving behind the non-ascendants.

The ones advocating for this solution, thought that the non-ascendants would get a second chance in the fourth elevation cycle. Nobody really knew the effects of leaving behind the underdeveloped lower leveled soul races, and most feared that they would not get a second chance but would be pulled entirely out, which actually were not in the interest of anybody. However since the soul races were so skilled in genetic sciences the anti-elevation factions (the ones against letting things go their natural course) felt that this standpoint was uncalled for because the genetics could be altered, if only they had more time.

Nevertheless, the pro-elevation faction (the ones supporting the natural elevation cycles) did not want to wait and argued against this according to the laws of the evolution cycles and the catching up mechanism these entailed, securing that all would eventually reach the same goal, if not in this cycle then in the next. This divided the soul races into two camps of dissimilar standpoints of unprecedented strength.

The dissimilarity in standpoint generated a new type of genetics, based upon the known types of genetics; the insectoid (HRF1) and the avian, the reptoid, the mammal (HRF2) as well as the higher levels of the mammal (HRF3) and the pre-stages of the true human genetics (HRF4). The humanoids holding the new genetics could have stayed in the HM as new possibilities generating new probability fields and eventually new soul races with HRFs connected hereto. Even though the two factions – representing a new type of genetics and the original version - could have solved their issues, the anti-elevation factions did not stop there; they went the full length having grown tired of the pro-elevation factions that always were two steps above them and therefore sort of set the stage of the lower evolutions, through their meta-council orders, to a growing dismay of the lower leveled races.

So the HRF2-HRF4s and some of the HRF5 meta-council members rioted and the dismay created a further alteration in the genetics of the anti-elevation races which led to a division of the HRFs between the anti-elevation soul races and the pro-elevation soul races.

The anti-elevation genetics with light coding and underdeveloped light units, generated the foundation of the less-progressive universe (still inside the holographic metaverse) where the anti-elevation factions were pulled to and the rest of the holographic metaverse remained as it was holding the pro-elevation factions. The division of the holographic metaverse happened because of the diversity of the light coding in the genetics, the lower level of light units and the polarization of the genetics from the present holographic resonance fields. A HRF can only hold genetics which resonance with the core principles in that HRF and if these differ, the genetics and their humanoids are pulled to new HRFs matching their genetics or the HM generates new HRFs to match the new genetic. The foundation of the less-progressive universe and the HM now ran on dissimilar HRFs and the division had come to stay. If all genetics were restored back to the original setting and quanta of light units, the two verses (the less-progressive universe and the holographic metaverse) would unite into one unified holographic metaverse again. Yet most of the anti-elevation factions wanted the division and a solitary universe of their own. They were controlled by the wish to continue the work with the new version of soul races, i.e. the less-progressive races, utilizing their skills in genetic manipulation to create new levels of probabilities and possibilities.

The anti-elevation factions mobilized a new version of the third elevation cycle run by genetic manipulation and TEGs, and they became less and less interested in returning to the original settings. They wanted to extend the existence of the less-progressive universe until the third elevation cycle of the metaverse were over to ensure that the less-progressive races would remain safe inside the gridworks of the LPU. The rest of the holographic metaverse could undergo the uplifting into the fourth elevation cycle and the less-progressive races would remain safe within their prolonged third elevation cycle, which they had put on hold by altering the genetics as well as the HRFs, that now ran on a slightly diverse setting, separating it from the main core principles of the holographic metaverse, or at least made the pull of the natural cycles less strong inside the less-progressive universe.

The Separation from the Holographic Metaverse
The less-progressive races began to settle into the HRFs of the less-progressive universe, building new settlements. To sustain their HRFs, the less-progressive races generated an artificial core in HRF5 of the LPU, called the central sun, to fuel the HRFs with the energies they needed to survive. Being cut off from the main core principles of the HM - the choice of creating a new type of universe that did not follow

the pull of the evolutionary cycles had energetically placed them to a halt - demanded a new source to sustain their HRFs.

The central sun was (and is) based upon the principles of the previous oversoul cycles, which were (and are) still in play in the HM due to the transition dynamics. To this core a certain amount of the principles from the present oversoul cycles were added, making it possible for the light coding to keep the principles of life, the light units, *inside* the light coding instead of instigating the transformation process. The central sun consists of less-progressive principles based upon an early version of *reversed* light coding. The reversing runs on one third of the original progression dynamics, which means that the less-progressive HRFs do and can evolve, although slowly, and not de-evolve.

For a long time the less-progressive races, now unfolding the HRFs of the less-progressive universe (the LPU), focused on building their preferred manifestations and to match the central sun energetically, they invented technologies to change the original holographic form with its soul genetics. The new technologies made it possible to pull reversed light coding from the central sun into their holographic form through the heart vortex just like it was done in the holographic metaverse.

In the holographic metaverse the soul races create a form directly from the soul genetics by pulling in the light coding from the HRF they want to work in and by linking up to the core principles of that field from the heart vortex. A form is changeable according to the energies that are pulled in as well as changes according to the development of the soul genetics. This still stands for the soul races of the holographic metaverse. However since the core principles of the less-progressive races had become artificial and based upon pre-consciousness energy of the previous oversoul cycle, they had to invent new forms that could keep in the soul genetics and by this preventing them from returning to the holographic metaverse or shed off the energies and return to the unified consciousness field.

To begin with, the less-progressive races continued the production of the technologically enhanced genetics that were developed before the division and added more features to the soul genetics by altering the fusion rate of the light coding and the light units. This generated a new type of light coding that suited the less-progressive races well. The new light coding of the body was dynamic and held many of the features of the original holographic changeable form, although to match the artificial central sun, it had to have a higher ratio of light coding from the previous oversoul cycles. The holographic form of the metaverse had the opposite as in a higher ratio of light units and less light coding to ensure the ability to transform. The less-progressive races therefore generated the LPU light coding and the substances that came out of it, which were used as the building material in the new areas and in the LPU energy systems utilized to create forms and bodies. The two verses were now fully separated.

The gel-like plasma matter of the first form of the less-progressive races in the higher areas of the LPU contained a high ratio of light coding with a smaller amount of soul genetics; i.e. the morphogenetic field had a higher level of the altered radiation energies, emitting light just like plasma do. The higher area less-progressive races took on the plasma matter to be their new form, and from here they linked up to the central sun unfolding a flow of energies, called *khundarays*.[12]

The higher leveled plasma races worked hard to create a suitable type of energy system and container for the soul races that had joined them in the division with the objective of making it possible for them to stay in the preferred HRFs in the lower areas of the new

---

[12] Named the seven rays in the theosophical teachings.

universe. Most of the deflected soul races from the third elevation cycle had lost their original holographic form during the division and were in dire need of a new form if they were to stay in the less-progressive universe. The higher leveled plasma races solved the affair by creating holographic forms, holding dissimilar ratios of light coding reversed slightly to keep in the soul genetics, i.e. the orb of the deflected soul races, as well as being able to link up to the central sun through the khundarays. The khundarays of the central sun were extended to produce gridworks in the lower areas of the LPU enabling the individual energy system to pull in the needed light coding of the central sun to keep the quantum morphogenetic field fueled with light coding. The variations in gridworks and their energy systems generated new holographic fields called *reality fields* and the LPU was now linked together as one system consisting of gridworks[13], reality fields, energy systems and TEGs fueled by the khundarays. The HRFs slowly altered into the new type of reality fields.

The higher leveled plasma races, i.e. the less-progressive reality field five races (the LPRF5s) were the founder races (the founding fathers) of the less-progressive universe (the LPU) as well as the creators of the lower leveled races of the LPU, i.e. the first LPRF4s,[14] the LPRF3s and the first LPRF2s. All of these races are the ancestors of all present day stellar races. The less-progressive races had now succeeded in generating both a new type of universe as well as forms where the genetics could evolve in a slower pace and at the same time keep up the properties of the light coding of the third elevation cycle.

The first less-progressive races were benign in nature and focused on enjoying the altered and slowed down type of universe they now

---

[13] The gridworks generate the dimensional bridges in the LPU a humanoid can link up to the bridges via the khundarays in the energy system as well as via the genetics.

[14] LPRF4s: Less-Progressive Reality Field Four races etc.

unfolded in. Many of them worked diligently on how to unfold new forms of the old type of energies and worshipped the Source, as they named the central sun and the khundarays that flowed from it, in temples and they built communities where the old type of principles were revered and honored as the Source of all there is, the life-giver and producer of life.

Over time as the memoires of the holographic metaverse and the link to the oversoul cycles vanished in the communities of the LPRF2s and the LPRF3s, and eventually the central sun became *the Source*.

The understanding of the holographic metaverse as the mother unfolding in the seven evolutionary cycles and the consciousness units as the seed of the father, generating the child, i.e. the soul and its form, slowly vanished and the stories of the LPRF5 founding races became fused with the new understandings of things. It then became known that Source had emanated into the founding fathers, which then became creators of all races, operating on behalf of the Source and unfolding the will of the prime creator.

Collaborations between the LPU and HM

Eventually the races of the two verses got accustomed to the new set up. It was a simple fact that the fifth evolutionary cycle had got a twist to the original plan of the cycle, leaving a division of the soul races stuck in the third elevation cycle in a whole new universe and the remaining races of the holographic metaverse to continue into the fourth elevation cycle. The fourth *elevation* cycle of the major fifth *evolutionary* cycle is the cycle where the soul races are to get all of their animal genetics transformed to be able to produce the true human genetics and by this take on a higher energetic type of form having the HRF4 as the lowest leveled resonance fields, getting ready to transit into the 6th evolutionary cycle through the remaining minor fifth, sixth and seventh elevation cycles.[15] In the third elevation cycle the light coding is transformed via the animal genetics getting ready to be able to hold the light units of the true human soul genetics. The races of the two verses had agreed to continue to collaborate since they came from the same metaverse. The collaboration was instigated by the LPRF5s and LPRF4s that still remembered and the LPRF3s acted as intermediaries between the higher LPU reality fields and the LPRF2s. As things progressed in the metaverse and the higher reality fields of the less-progressive universe, new solutions were needed to meet the demand of the issues of the LPRF2 races that slowly but surely got stuck in the evolution of the animal genetics within the level 2 reality fields of the less-progressive universe. Most of the LPRF2s had forgotten all about the goal of the third elevation cycle and would get lost if nothing was done to assist them.

---

[15] There are seven elevation cycles in each large evolutionary cycle in the metaverse.

The LPRF3 Sirian Workstations

Meanwhile as *the LPRF2s* (insectoid, avian and lower reptoid races in different combinations holding TEGs) stood still in their progression, other things happened on the LPRF3 level among *the LPRF3 races* (higher developed reptoids and lower developed mammals holding TEGs) which functioned as a bridging principle between the higher leveled plasma races of *the LPRF4 races* (fully developed mammals holding small amounts of TEGs) and *LPRF5s* (almost none TEGs with soul genetics from the HM) and the rest of the LPU.

The present day 6th dimensional races of the DE2 are known as the Sirius A and Sirius B races;[16] however history has to be adjusted to the early facts of this binary system.[17] Originally Sirius was a LPRF3 cluster of stars unfolded from a mixed core with light units from the HM[18] and light coding from the LPU. The cluster functioned as workstations for the intermediary LPRF3s and the rest of the LPU as well as bridge zones to the HM. In other words the binary system did not exist to begin with.

The collaboration involving the higher leveled LPU races and the HRF3 and HRF4 races that did not deflect, unfolded into scientific projects attempting to solve some of the issues with the TEGs, which had a tendency to break down in spite of the khundarays gridwork infusions from the central sun, as well as keeping the bridge zones open for the ones who regretted their shift into the LPU. Actions to solve the issues of the non-evolving LPRF2s were also part of the

---

[16] The LPDE2 has holographic form in 4D, energy system in 5D and template in 6D; however there are variations to this.

[17] Ideas of Sirius being a trinary system have been debated since the 1995's but there is no Sirius C. Sirius C, when it was and is spotted, is a huge spaceship from the Sirian B races orbiting Sirius B.

[18] When I talk about the holographic metaverse, it is the HM. When I talk about the races from the HM, working inside the LPU reality fields it is the HMRFs. When the HM races later work inside the post-timeline event densities it is the HMDE3s etc. When the HM races evolve in their own settings, they are called HRF3s etc.

collaboration. The Sirian star cluster held variations of the LPRF3 and LPRF4 light coding and the light units from the HRF3 and HRF4 areas generating the mixed core for the purpose, and it was therefore the perfect working center for the collaboration. The mixed core both held the main core principles plus the reversed light coding of the central sun.

The Sirius Star Cluster

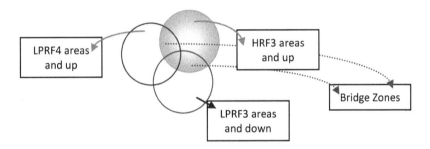

The LPRF3 Reptoid Settlements on Maldak

The mixed core generated a possibility for the HRF2 soul races of the holographic metaverse to enter the LPU and settle there. Some of the HRF2 races with the avian, reptoid and mammal soul genetics found pleasure in settling down in the LPU in the vicinity of the Sirian work-stations. The Sirian workstations held both HM races as well as LPU races. The races living in the Sirian workstations controlled and took care of the bridge zones and the new areas unfolding from the mixed core of the Sirian system, to call it that.

The possibilities for the HM soul races to take on a new type of form posed an interesting challenge for them and they became part of the workstations to explore the construction of the LPU energy system with the upper template holding the dormant genetics, not to be utilized in the areas they had entered and the lower template that connected them to the khundarays gridworks and by this provided them with an LPU form. The three main vortexes held the genetics they had chosen to activate in the LPU body were also exciting them.

The upper triangle generating a personality unfolded from the integrated genetics was also an thrilling new possibility for the HRF2 races since the original HM form did not have these divisions and differences in light coding (energy) and light units (soul genetics) and therefore the new energy system posed a challenge to master for the HRF2 races.[19] Many also found the reality fields of the Sirian system intriguing and wanted to unfold their possibilities and probabilities there and thus new areas, matching the HRF2 avian, reptoid and mammal genetics were generated. The first settlements were created on what we call Maldak (naturally it was called something else back then); a reality field positioned in the vicinity of the Sirian system.

The reptoid settlements on Maldak were generally uncomplicated in their set up. The HRF2 reptoid races that unfolded there held a high percentage of mammal genetics, given the fact that the reptoid HRF2 races had elevated and now mostly belonged to the fourth elevation cycle of the HM and therefore they took on the human form as we know it, although they were taller. The best resemblance is the depictions of the gods from Valhalla. The stories of Valhalla are a mythological remnant of the HRF2 reptoid-mammal settlements on Maldak. The Maldakian races were benevolent in nature, i.e. the Asgard strain having mostly tall blonde human looking features.[20] However due to the reptoid genetics, they could turn into warriors,

---

[19] The HM body consists of three interchangeable versions, where the genetics are integrated directly: The radiation body based upon the radiation field and its light units, the vibration body based upon the vibration field and its light units and the HM light coding form matching the reality field where the united holographic resonance system unfolds its potentials.
[20] The Maldakian races of the early settlements have been blended into the stories of the Lyrans, as I see it.

which some of them did during the Reptilian Riots. The Maldakian races preferred the work with agriculture, farming and associated growth potentials of plantlife that could unfold into the new settlements on Maldak. The plantlife on Maldak was naturally not what we see today, but light coding holding small amounts of light units and thus unfolding plantlife that actually were a lifeform, with a radiation and vibration field able to process the core principles into life but also conscious existence. During the solidification process of the timeline event, these lifeforms perished and turned into dust; hence the bare surface of the Moon which the remnants of Maldak turned into during the timeline event.

The LPRF3 Avian Settlements on Mars

Contrary to the Maldakian settlement the Martian settlement held LPRF2 avian races from the LPU (again the reality field was not called Mars back then). The LPRF2 avians had got LPRF3 TEGs added to be able to exist inside the LPRF3 areas. Most of them were ready to enter the LPRF3 level of genetics and thus the TEGs only amplified the existing possibilities in them. The LPRF2 avians looked less human and more humanoid, given that they had light to dark blue skin, avian facial features and a smaller thin body resembling an upright bird but without the feathers for most part; some did have tiny soft feathers with rainbow coloration. Naturally the torso was not as big as we see it in birds on our planet because the avians on Mars did not have the capacity to fly and thus were in no need of the great bundle of muscles in the torso.

The Martian avians were cleaver and scientific by nature, due to the higher ratio of TEGs. The TEGs enabled them to function in the Sirius system although on the lower levels. The Martian settlements unfolded all sorts of scientific laboratories and spacecraft landing stations and became the center of technological innovations, trade of

51

TEGs and sciences in the Sirius system. As the Sirius system grew in size and the settlements grew along with it, other races joined the collaboration of the HM and the LPU. When I say other HM races, it becomes difficult to understand, because are there not only two verses? No, there are many verses unfolded from the holographic metaverse as the genetics developed and generated reality fields. The HM holographic resonance fields had undergone, in the time of the Sirius system, a gigantic progression and development during the fourth elevation cycle and many new HRF races had unfolded from the time when the Internal Strife took place.[21] However this is out of our scope of events, since our goal is to cover the events that led to our reality field and present state of being.

The LPRF3 Sirius System with the new
settlements of Maldak, Er'th and Mars

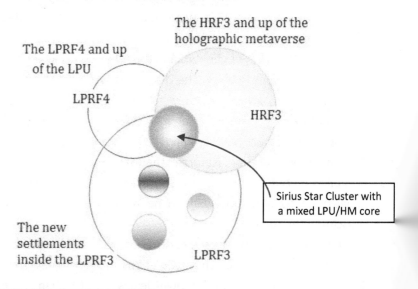

The HRF3 and up of the
holographic metaverse

The LPRF4 and up
of the LPU

LPRF4

HRF3

Sirius Star Cluster with
a mixed LPU/HM core

The new
settlements
inside the LPRF3

LPRF3

---

[21] Many of these distant races are yet to be encountered as we re-activate our soul genetics and through the genetics, regain the telepathic contact with the new HRF races of the fourth elevation cycle, all holding a higher ratio of true human genetics.

The LPRF3 Er`Th Colonies

Whereas the Martian settlements focused on the TEGs and all of the wonders the TEGs could be utilized in from steering spacecrafts to controlling all sorts of scientific sub-fields by a mix of light coding, the gridworks and TEGs, the Maldakian settlements investigated the basic lifeforms of plants and small animals and the elemental evolution of consciousness.

The next step for the races present in the Sirius system was to collaborate in investigating the LPU humanoid form and its energy system to higher levels of progression as assistance to the halted LPRF2s but also to the rest of the LPU races. The upper and lower templates with the vortexes were as such a rough model of something that could be much more sophisticated and the Sirian councils of the participating races in the Sirius system joined forces in a project to generate more advanced LPU forms and energy systems, which were able to shift into the higher and lower areas of the LPU as a natural thing or by consciousness alone. At the time of the Er'Th[22] colonies the LPU forms and energy systems could only shift into higher areas by inserting TEGs and other forms of modification.

The Er'Th colonies became the place for this project and were in its initial state when the timeline event happened. The Er'Th colonies had all the racial blueprints ready, the gridworks and the light coding of the khundarays were set in place to unfold new LPU forms and energy systems as well as the laboratories, the sciences and all of what was needed to make the LPU genetics and TEGs grow into viable forms able to fit the new version of the LPU form. All things needed to make a reality field unfold a certain type of setting were in place as well as the next generation of light coding and light units built upon the mixed core principles of the Sirius system. Since the LPRF3s, i.e.

---

[22] Er'Th: Energy, rays, technology, holographic forms.

the old HRF3 races that deflected, had a smaller quantity of TEGs and a higher percentage of mammal genetics they had brought with them from the HM, compared to the lower leveled LPRF races, they held most of the original information from the HM as well as the ability to link up to the core principles, if they chose so.

The LPRF3s were thus appointed the custodians or the guardians of the bridge zones of the Sirius system as well as the overseers of the initiatives carried out on the Er'Th colonies that eventually would sustain the other lower leveled areas of the LPU.

However the project was not up and completely running when the timeline event took place.

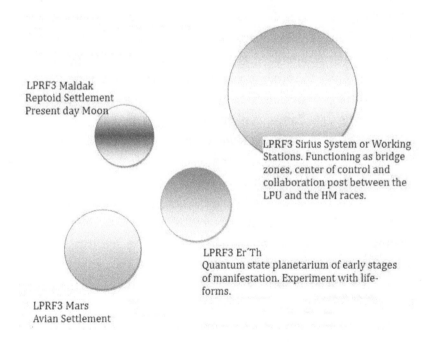

LPRF3 Maldak
Reptoid Settlement
Present day Moon

LPRF3 Sirius System or Working Stations. Functioning as bridge zones, center of control and collaboration post between the LPU and the HM races.

LPRF3 Er'Th
Quantum state planetarium of early stages of manifestation. Experiment with life-forms.

LPRF3 Mars
Avian Settlement

The Timeline Event

What circumstances led to the merging of gridworks and TEGs? That is the question we are to answer in this part, because this catastrophe is the reason for all new races in the LPU as well as the dark ones. The dark ones originated from the Sirian workstations from one of the scientific laboratories positioned there.

Due to the mixed core, connecting the HM and the LPU into a unified system on a LPRF3 level, some of the workstations were the place where scientific work were performed to undo the breakdown of the TEGs by experimenting on the ratio that would keep the TEGs from breaking down. The collapsing TEGs had a tendency to generate a sort of dark substance that literally ate up the light coding of the energy system and it was highly infectious as well. This understanding caused great distress to the higher leveled plasma races, because their creation was literally breaking down from within.

The LPU higher leveled plasma races had long preferred to isolate themselves in the cleaner and less messy areas of the LPU, in an attempt to keep their original genetics as pure as possible and only utilizing very small amounts of TEGs. The higher leveled plasma races knew the imperfections of the TEGs and for that reason they did not put themselves in harm's way by inserting larger amounts of TEGs; they only integrated the needed percentage to keep them phased in to the central sun as well as connecting them to the khundarays, keeping their holographic form alive. Both the HM races and the LPU races, taking part in the Sirian workstations, understood that an 80-20 ratio was needed to keep the soul genetics from the holographic metaverse intact. If only the LPU energy system held no more than 20 percent of TEGs, the remaining 80 percent of the soul genetics would stay clear of the infection and the TEGs would not break down.

The more this shifted into a 50-50 ratio, the more easily the inserted TEGs were to break down and turn the energy system dark. If this happened, the upper and lower template (the template with the dormant original genetics as well as the gridwork template) would go into deterioration. The deterioration of the upper and lower template would lead to a separation from the HM and eventually the LPU, pulling the infected energy system and TEGs having no connection to the khundarays etc., into separate reality fields[23] where the infected energy systems and TEIGs would dissolve slowly on their own. This was seen as the first solution to the infection; i.e. to let nature run its course and let the humanoids carrying the infection, be pulled into new reality field, i.e. the dark areas, where they would live until evaporation.

Naturally some of the LPRF3s could not resist experimenting with the TEIGs in the hope of solving the problem of the dark areas. At first a selected area of gridworks of the workstation was infected to see how the infection acted upon the gridwork, since the dark areas slowly began the same deterioration process as the infected energy systems living there, which could lead to infected gridworks across the borders of the dark areas. Then a portion of the central sun light coding (plasma core flows) was infected with a set of TEIGs to see how much it would take to restore the dark substance. Even though the plasma core flows had been contained within a core plasma crystal (holographic container for light coding) the infection got out of control and infected the entire crystal and from there it jumped from

---

[23] If the genetics change and exceed the settings of the HRFs or reality field they are part of and no other reality field is a match to them, they are pushed out and begin to generate a new reality field, where they can unfold their new features. This is how new realities are generated.

the core plasma crystal into the ones working with the experiments, through the khundarays connection. From the infected LPRF3s, the infection spread into the workstation and from there into the core of the Sirian star cluster holding the mixed LPU reversed light coding and HM core principles.

The adding of the infection to a selected area of the gridworks in the workstation, the infected humanoids living there undergoing the separation process into the dark ones, as well as a portion of the core of the Sirian star cluster, which had turned into a dark zone, initiated a series of timeline collapses, where the gridworks and their timelines began to break down as the TEIGs spread out through the gridworks, the LPRF3s and their genetics, deteriorating all.

The timeline event began as a domino effect of the infected areas and LPRF3 humanoids into the timelines they were connected to and from here jumped to the reality fields themselves. Due to the laws of how genetics, timelines and reality fields work together, the new features of the genetics and their adjacent reality fields began the separation process from the existing gridwork they belonged to, as well as the transition into dark areas.

The splitting off generated a huge burst of forces, because of the HM core principles reacting to the separation, pushing more of the infected reversed light coding into the core in a sort of feedback chain-reaction. The response to this change of the dynamics in the mixed core of the Sirian star cluster was to begin a resetting, which is an inbuilt safety mechanism of all reality fields and HRFs that stray too far away from the original principles; i.e. either the genetics are pushed into a new field, if they do not match the one they are part of, or the field resets from a core level and out, forcing the genetics of the humanoids present there to reset back to the original settings of the field. The Sirian star cluster and the workstations underwent a huge transformation during the timeline event. The cluster merged into one field of infected plasma core flows, distorted khundarays, infected timelines, gridworks and reality fields as well as dissolving the present LPRF3 races into bits. The timeline event created new reality fields, consisting of densities and dimensions and unfolded a whole new species of humanoids.

Most of the HM races were pulled out and back to their original status because of the resetting mechanism in their section of the mixed core with the original principles, which they were linked up to. This literally saved the most of the soul races in the workstations even though they were reset to the level they entered the HM with. The ones that did not make it, due to full integration into the LPU energy system, were fragmented along with the LPU races and their soul genetics were fused into the new species of humanoids.

The Ancient Stellar Races

The binary stellar system Sirius A and Sirius B were created since the unified Sirian star cluster separated due to the infected gridworks, where the Sirius B held the most changed levels. However the effect did not stop there given that all of the reality fields of the Sirius star cluster, including the LPRF3 settlements on Maldak, Mars and Er'th had been affected by the explosion-split-resetting dynamics, which had changed the core plasma flows in these reality fields of the LPU, generating a boundary of dissimilar phasing of the LPU khundarays and light coding, pushing the non-affected higher areas of the LPU away from the LPRF3 areas and below. The reality fields linked up to the Sirius star cluster had changed into a new kind of dimensionality, holding a new variety of the slightly reversed light coding of the LPU bearing a new type of TEGs predisposed for the infection as an inbuilt part of the light coding (the TEGs were now merged into the light coding as a non-removable feature). The remaining LPRF3s, both the ones carrying the predisposed TEGs changed from what we know as the less-progressive races into a new type of humanoids known as *the ancient stellar races* or the forefathers of the new stellar races. The ancient stellar races unfolded from the timeline event as two main lineages; one holding the properties of the predisposed merged-in TEGs and a faction holding a minor level of merged-in TEGs but without the predisposition for the infection, i.e. the possibility the TEGs to break down. The faction with the predisposed TEGs became the reptoid-mammal Sirian B lineages, of which there are many races today, and the faction still having the golden ratio of 80 percent original genetics, albeit now the 20 percent were merged-in TEGs, unfolded as the Sirian As.

After the timeline event the previous mixed core, now distorted, retracted into a "black hole". The core plasma flows, which had got the infection to begin with, along with the retracted distorted core, were turned into an antagonistic core in the 8th dimension unfolding the dynamics of dark plasma rays. The infected gridworks linked up to the antagonistic core pulled the other dark areas closer expanding the dark areas. The renewed dark areas inhabited the infected genetics from the Sirian star cluster during the explosion-split-resetting event, i.e. the genetics from the scientists that got infected and initiated the splitting off to begin with.

During the timeline event the infected scientists got their upper and lower template ripped off and only the infected energy system, with the genetics they held at the moment of the event, remained in them along with the infected TEGs. This LPRF3 faction, with their dark areas and dark plasma rays, became the leaders (the masters) of the dark ones given that they, after the merging with the existing dark areas, took leadership of all that were in them. Most of the LPRF3 dark ones were clever scientists, creators of TEGs, manipulators of light coding and held a high degree of information and knowledge of the original principles.

The upper leveled LPU races, i.e. the LPRF4 and up, were cut off from the lower areas of the LPU due to the new dimensional settings of the LPRF3 as well as the new version of the reversed light coding. The new coding literally repulsed the original reversed light coding of the khundarays of the central sun and with this, the races connected to it. The distorted dimensions of the LPU became the dark areas (the dark LPRF3s), holding the LPRF3 antagonistic core, fueling the TEIGs in a new way with dark energy, dark energy systems with the merged-in TEIGs[24] as well as the divided Sirius system, bridging the Sirius B to the dark areas and the Sirian A to the rest of the LPU. The Sirian As are not strongly represented in our story since they linked up to the HM shortly after the timeline event and created the HMDE3 areas, out of our reach genetically and telepathically, leaving behind small groups of descendants in the remaining non-infected LPRF3 reality fields. The HMDE3 areas are linked up to the HRFs of the holographic metaverse and thus very difficult for all LPUs to reach.

Below the transformed and distorted LPRF3 system, now called the density three systems (the DE3s), a new form of density two (the DE2s) slowly unfolded, due to the changes of the khundarays and gridworks activated by the boundary of dissimilar phasing between the LPRF4s and the former LPRF3s. The connection to the central sun became more distant, because the gridworks and genetics had to pass through the boundary of dissimilar phasing, which was not easy.

The DE3s and DE2s were de facto sealed off from the rest of the LPU and this changed the reality fields further as well as the ancient stellar races living there, undergoing the transition along with the reality fields. Not much is known of these ancient races among the new stellar races, only that the ancient races are the forefathers of the present day new stellar races and that they unfolded from the

---

[24] I have not talked much about the dark DE3 areas since there is no use of this. It exists and as you know, what you focus on you give energy.

two lineages of the Sirius system,[25] giving the gene pool to all of the races we know of today in our system.

The post-timeline event reality fields mainly unfolded in the density two (DE2) areas since the density three (DE3) were either pulled into the HMDE3 area under the Sirian As, had turned dark, had been pushed into other dimensions or had turned into the Sirius B system, which due to the infected TEGs and small amounts of soul genetics dropped in vibrational level and merged into the density two systems on a 6th dimensional level. From this position of the highest level of the DE2s, the Sirian B systems later on took on the role as the overseers, claiming the pre-timeline event rights as the guardians from the Sirian workstations, controlling the new stellar races of the DE2D6s and the DE2D4s reality fields, housing the descendants of the ancient stellar races with the merged-in TEGs, being to a degree artificial and yet holding some level of the soul genetics.

The Creation of the DE1D3 Solar System

What once was one of the workstations had now become a brown dwarf in the transformed Sirius system. The binary stars arose as the main reality fields of the previous LPRF3 system and the workstations closest to the explosion had undergone a conglomeration into one large planet, which we see as Jupiter.[26] The remnants of the exploding workstation were gathered together in the outskirts of the fusion field, generating what we know as the Asteroid Belt. The reality fields Er´Th and Maldak had been remodeled into reality fields with a more solidified holographic setting and pushed into their present positions

---

[25] The Sirius A lineage is known as the lineage of wisdom and compassion and the Sirian B as the lineage of technology and sciences.

[26] Saturn, Pluto and Uranus belong to other reality fields and have been generated or brought into the solar system after the timeline event. Venus and Mercury could be remnants of the explosion. I have little or no information regarding these two planets for some reason. To me they seem like dead planetoids.

generating what we call Earth and the Moon. The reality field of Mars had turned into a stony and sandy planet where all the prior thriving communities were desolated to the ground. Whatever materials that were left on Mars had been calcified and "frozen in time" in weird formations of burned off stony materials. Er'Th and Maldak had undergone a metamorphosis where the two reality fields had merged and then were then pulled apart again, changing the properties of both reality fields. Er'Th had changed from a pre-matter quantum state into a reality field incapsuled in ice and rocky materials, pushing the LPU quantum state into a sub-reality field between the 3rd and 4th dimension, leaving behind an unstable holographic reality with a forever changing surface. Maldak had lost its original features and had become a bare planetoid with little resemblance to the green fruitful reality field[27] it used to be.

Flow patterns in Earth's core

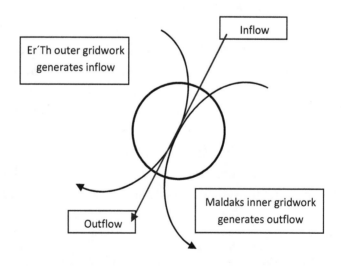

___

[27] A reality field holds the holographic properties making it non-solid and changeable according to the genetics present there. A planet is solid and as such un-changeable.

The process of the solidification tells its own story in the soil and rock sediments where the changes, from a positive quantum state into a planet with a geomagnetic core, are seen as hundreds of thousands of years of geological changes with pole shifts, tectonic plate shifts and volcanic activity generating the crust.

Earth was able to develop an environment for new lifeforms, with a bit of help from the ancient stellar races and their technologies, in contrast to the other planets, because of the former colonies, holding the blueprints for new LPU lifeforms and genetics in the gridworks as possibilities of new types of energy systems. The outer levels of the core of Earth thus consist of the gridwork of Er´Th, still connected to the reality field of Sirius A[28] and an inner core connected to the residual gridwork of Maldak (present day Moon), which for a short period during the dimensional fusion became one with Er´Th.[29] Earth and the Moon are interconnected through the core of Earth, as well as connected to the Sirius system, both on a Sirius B level (because of the Moon) and on a Sirius A level.

The Ancient Stellar Colonies on DE1D3

But before the ancient stellar races disappeared and evolved into the later stellar races, initiatives were instigated to solve the problems that had arisen after the timeline event in the LPRF3s but also to take advantage of the new planet of Earth.

The holographic blueprints of the new LPU energy systems (from the Er´Th colonies) merged into the gridworks of a changeable reality field, in a messy solidified way, was something entirely new and had to be investigated further. Thus programs were set in motion to bring up a new humanoid lifeforms as well as surroundings (via 12 crystal

---

[28] Jupiter is linked up to the Sirius gridwork as well.
[29] On the fundamental level, the Moon and Earth consist of the same elemental building blocks. If the Moon had an atmosphere it would be as inhabitable as Earth.

pillars, which generated an inhabitable environment) where the new bodies, energy systems and type of mind could unfold, holding the genetics of all races. These programs were directed by the HRF3 races and the DE3 Sirian A races, being linked up to the HM in DE3 (through a remnant gridwork holding the original LPRF3 light coding) and this collaboration was the first to enter the DE1D3 solar system. The collaboration unfolded as five colonies, scattered around the planet Earth.[30]

The five colonies were called:

- *The Pleiadian Colonies, known as the owners of the Silver Star gridwork of consciousness and energy linking up to the dimensional bridge of the many in the DE2D5 region (before the reptilian takeover).*

- *The avian Arcturian Colonies, known as the owners of the Falcon gridwork of consciousness and energy linking to the dimensional bridge of the few in the DE2D4 region.*

- *The Collaboration of the Distant Races from two reality fields outside our present capability of understanding, were the owners of two un-named gridworks of consciousness and energy linking to the dimensional bridges of the advanced in the DE2D6 regions.*

- *The Ancient Travelers from the Realms of the Beginning, known as the owners of the Lion gridwork of consciousness and energy linking to the bridge zones into the HRF3.*

---

[30] I call it Earth to distinguish from Er'Th, i.e. the original reality field that gave the blueprints to our planet.

The Ancient Pleiadian Colonies

First and foremost the ancient Pleiadian colonies do not denote a race that stem from the present day 5D new stellar system, we know as the Pleiades.[31] The present day Pleiades are mammal-reptoid races are part of the draco-reptilian areas.[32] The ancient Pleiadians stem from the first DE2D5 reptoid-mammal races[33] and descend from the lineage of Sirius A. The ancient Pleiadians had seven co-councils, of which we know their names as the seven sisters in the mythology. Each of the co-councils, given that the first Pleiadian system was a collective and functioned as one united reality field,[34] presided over a section of the collective and the races that took part in the DE1D3 colonies came from the areas under the co-councils of Maia. Their goal, along with the Sirian As, was to generate a humanoid form that was able to exist in the middle DE1D3 areas and grow this humanoid form into a skilled caretaker of the gridworks (and blueprints) of the areas, as well as an important co-worker in the development of the DE2s back to a standard that was able to access the DE3 areas.

They wanted to generate a humanoid form that could battle the infection as well as utilize the first generation of TEGs from the HM. The first generation of TEGs held larger amounts of HM light coding and soul genetics than the later versions that were generated inside the LPU, where the soul genetics had to be fragmented and modified

---

[31] This group is under the reptilian leadership and hold mammal-reptoid genetics.

[32] A mammal-reptoid race is an original mammal race added with reptoid TEGs mostly done by the draco-reptilian overlords and the scientific draconians. Dracos are partly avian but mostly reptilian in genetic set up.

[33] Reptoid-mammal races are original reptoids, who have evolved into holding mammal genetics.

[34] In contrast of today, where the reptilians administer the stellar system from the Alcyone system and the councils to collaborate under their leadership. A minority of the old Maian-Pleiadians exists in the vicinity to the DE2D5 areas bordering up to the HM and the DE2D6 Sirian As. Due to differences in genetics, the reptilian cannot enter the reality fields of the Maian-Pleiadians or the Sirian As.

to at all link up to the artificial central sun. The TEGs from the mixed core of the LPRF3 Sirius system were gone or had broken down during the timeline event. Therefore the DE1D3 system were the last place, where the blueprint of the first generation of TEGs existed, rested dormant and intact in the gridworks of the DE1D3, making it a very valuable place to have control over if the knowledge of how to work with the gridworks as well as how to activate and unfold the blueprints into energy systems and viable functional genetics, were part of the genetic setup. The Sirian As had the knowledge from the LPRF3 Er´Th colonies and through the Maia-Pleiadians[35] the goal was to invoke the blueprints and build a colony where the new humanoid form could reset, re-grow and self-heal through the use of the first generation of TEGs added with Sirian A/Maia-Pleiadians genetics.

One faction of the Maia-Pleiadians settled in the DE1D3, holding the genetic and telepathic connection to the supreme councils of Sirius A. This faction was appointed the leading council of all that took place by the other races present on the DE1D3 system and when they went into hiding with the true earth humanoid DE1D3s and the HMDE3 Sirian A, they became the councils of the avian-mammal RWBs, who later joined the cause.

The Ancient Arcturian Colonies
The ancient Arcturians are not the same as the new stellar races of Arcturians (the Arcs) of today. The Arcs hold high levels of TEGs giving them access to the DE3D7 areas, where they have generated reality fields that are able to house them above the distorted areas as well as far away from the LPRF3 dark areas. The Arcs have created worlds built upon technologies and artificial gridworks phased dimensionally a bit higher than the distorted LPRF3 (the dark DE3) gridworks, and

---

[35] The Sirian As cannot work in the DE2 areas due to their higher vibrating genetics.

66

resemble to a high degree any robotic scientific world we can think of, except that the Arcs are biological and have no wires, electronics or anything like that merged into their systems. The robotic similarity lies in the high level of TEGs. The ancient Arcturians came from the DE2D4 areas that arose after the timeline event. They held the second generation of the TEGs from the LPU; post-timeline TEGs as well as the original avian genetics from the factions that separated during the Internal Strife. The avians had from very early on, after they had got the new form from the higher leveled LPRF5s, minded their own business and generated their own reality fields in the lower areas of the LPU.

Some of the Arcturians had taken part of the Martian settlements due to their scientific knowledge, but most of the avian races had retracted to quiet settlements in the vicinity of the LPU, building communities where technology had been abandoned.

The avian communities outside the LPRF3 perimeter of the explosion were therefore not harmed by this. Unfortunately most of these communities were destroyed under the Reptilian Riots or were taken over by the DE2D5 draco-reptilian warlords with modified avian genetics enabling them to enter the communities.

The draco-reptilian warlord tricked or convinced the avians to take part in hijacking other areas. Most of these peaceful communities are now gone and the avian races have been modified into negatives, known as the avian-reptoids (winged snake or Nagasians) or avian-mammal humanoids resembling humans of Earth. Most of the avian-mammal races have worked or work as intermediaries between the draco-reptilian overlords and the races of the DE2D4. Some of the intermediary avian-mammals were instated into the middle DE1D3 areas after the takeover and became the brotherhood before the division into the LWBs and the RWBs. Today there are various DE2D4 races and not only the avians, albeit all hold either avian TEGs or avian genetics enabling them to exist in the DE2D4 areas. The avian Arcturians that took part of the new colonies were a small group that wanted to return to the HM and undo the changes of their LPU humanoid form and genetics. They had grown tired of the LPU and were ready to do the needed evolutionary steps, which would get them back into the fourth elevation cycle of the HM. Most of the Arcturians left the DE2D4 areas and settled in the DE1D3 to commit fully to the genetic modification, infusion and experiments that were needed to make it possible for them to return home.

The Arcturian settlers were all killed during the reptilian takeover of the DE1D3, considered by the draco-reptilians to be traitors and deflectors of the cause, i.e. what divided the holographic metaverse to begin with.

The Collaboration of Distant Races
The Collaboration of Distant Races was a colony housing DE2D6 races that had stepped down, by the use of a technology called dimensional blocking. Very little is known about them since they left the colonies quite early in the programs.

The Ancient Travelers from the Realms of the Beginning
The Ancient Travelers from the Realms of the Beginning came from the HRF3 areas, crossed the borders between the LPU and the HM to take part in the DE1D3 programs. They came offering HRF3 soul genetics to replace the genetics that had been lost in the timeline event. New soul genetics were needed to fully activate the new humanoid blueprint of the gridworks, as well as to be able to link up to the bridge zones between the DE1D3 areas and the HM.

They volunteered to stay and merge with the gridworks of the DE1D3 to keep the gridworks of the quantum flux fields fueled with soul genetics. This was a different solution than the one chosen in the

Sirian star cluster system, which had been based upon a mixed core of LPU light coding and HM light units. The mixed core had unfolded the gridworks needed to house the HM races. Here the HRF3s chose to stay, becoming the HMDE3s, connect to the humanoid blueprint in the gridworks[36] and by this securing that the gridworks never stopped having the correct level of soul genetics needed to bridge to the HM.

The HMDE3s settled in an area named the Hyperborean isle, which will rise again as the middle DE1D3 areas reset to the initial settings, i.e. the setting of the colonies. The HMDE3 settlement is for the present hidden in a secured area called Hallow Earth. Hallow Earth is not a correct name, but the area got this name by some theosophists re-activating the memories of the first landmasses of this planet holding a very highly evolved race not from this planet.

The Three Main Programs of the DE1D3

1) The creation of a true earth humanoid overseen and instigated by the Maia-Pleiadians/Sirian As.

2) Regeneration of fragmented genetics from the timeline event, as well as experiments to solve some of the issues with the distorted gridworks, preventing the LPU races from returning to the HM. This became the Restoration Program under the avian Arcturians.

3) The Rehabilitation Program was set in motion to lift the issues with the rehabilitation of the merged-in infected and non-infected TEGs from the timeline event as an attempt to avoid the dark areas to grow further, also under the Arcturians as well as the distant travelers in the beginning of the program.

---

[36] New humanoids, in generated reality fields, can only unfold if their racial blueprint is imprinted into the gridwork. When the racial genetics change and a humanoid is transferred to a new gridwork, the first humanoid will imprint the gridwork with the racial blueprint.

The DE1D3 True Earth Humanoid Program

The DE1D3 humanoid program has to stay a secret to us until after the resetting back into the settings of the original colonies. The Maia-Pleiadians present in our reality field today have asked this of me. The reason is that we, in our present version, are not able to utilize the possibilities of our original humanoid form, i.e. the form of this reality field. We are barely able to use the little possibilities we have through the dimmed down chakra system, although connected to the astral barrier and controlled by this, it is still possible to free and activate it, and by this learn to utilize the technologies, which were installed in the true earth humanoid form.

The true earth humanoid form bridges the soul genetics, the first type of TEGs with a third type of genetics that were invented for the true earth humanoids alone. The third type of genetics has to stay hidden until after the full resetting of our planet because not until the gridworks of the Lion and the Silver Star are back up and running, are we able to reactivate this type of genetics and unfold our potentials through the assistance of the Maia-Pleiadians/Sirian As, or by internal knowledge. However we can begin the slow process of altering the DE1D3 energy system and the organic form to be able to link up to the true earth humanoid form after we have shed off this present form. Thus for now the other two programs have to suffice in our quest for the hidden treasures of the true earth humanoid form of DE1D3s. One thing can be said though to silence our questions: No, the reptoid-mammal bio-genetic set up[37] humans hold today is not the true earth humanoid form; the reptoid-mammal form is a genetic experiment done by the hijacking races after the Reptilian Riots under

---

[37] Some hold mammal-reptoid bio-genetics, i.e. mammal genetics added with reptoid TEGs in contrast to the reptoid-mammal bio-genetics, i.e. reptoid genetics added with mammal TEGs. Human bio-genetics are built from the integrated genetics of the level one energy system.

the draco-reptilian overlords. The reptoid-mammal form is their invention along with the prototypes of Grays and other insectoid-avian races, which were generated in the DE1D3 areas as well as on other similar reality fields, to be the caretakers of the various draco-reptilian experiments.

Most of the DE1D3 true earth humanoids were slaughtered during the takeover of the DE1D3s, and the ones that survived, retracted to Hallow Earth with the HMDE3s, from where they have been in contact with the RWBs since the division of the brotherhood.

The Restoration Program
The restoration program was instigated in the first stages of the colonies. It was a joined effort to solve some of the problems with the infected genetics from the explosion. The infected genetics and TEGs generated glitches in the gridworks of the density two fields, due to the separated state from the rest of the LPU because of the repulsing barrier between the LPRF4s and LPRF3s (now the DE3s). The DE1D3 energy system (the hara quadrant)[38] was invented to re-circulate light coding from and into the integrated genetics and TEGs of the LPU holographic energy system (LPUHES) by connecting the DE1D3 energy system to the gridworks of the DE1D3. The DE1D3 gridworks held the healing possibilities of the infused soul genetics from the HMDE3s.

Just by being present in the DE1D3 and linked up to its gridwork, by supplementing the LPUHES with the DE1D3 energy system – attached through the throat, heart and root vortexes – would be healing and restoring. The soul genetic infused gridworks activated the self-healing sequences in the fragmented or infected TEGs if the infection was not too massive.

---

[38] The hara quadrant is taught in the second year of the education and how to regain the function of it.

The chakras of the hara quadrant had a circumference of vibration light coding and a core holding radiation light coding. The two types of light coding generated the capability to interfere with the reality field the LPU holographic energy system (the level one energy system) was part of before it came to the DE1D3. Or the LPUHES could change into the settings of the next reality field, acquired to leave the DE1D3s after the restoration. It could also process the light coding of the HM, if needed.

The Important three Chakras Bridging the Two Energy Systems

The two Energy Systems and their interconnectedness

Main Center with
Upper Triangle

Throat Chakra in front of Throat Vortex

Thymus Chakra in front of Heart Vortex

Hara Chakra

Root Chakra in front of Root Vortex

The hara quadrant ensured a projection-action-reaction mechanism of the integrated genetics of the LPUHES that would activate and cleanse the similar energies in the gridworks of the DE2 and DE3 reality fields and by this repairing the genetics from the explosion to be able to turn back into the LPU settings from before the timeline event. When a DE2 or DE3 stellar humanoid entered the DE1D3s, still having its LPUHES, got the hara quadrant added and temporarily took on the DE1D3 humanoid form (which we do not know what was) in full or by projection, the healing and restoration mechanisms of the DE1D3 gridworks would affect back, as a sort of feed-back loop, to the reality field the stellar humanoid came from. This would happen in three steps by the merging of the two reality fields:

The first step was to merge the root chakra and root vortex connecting the gridworks of the lower template (holding the light coding of the reality field the LPUHES came from) to the quantum morphogenetic field connected to the first level of the hara quadrant and by this connecting the extra-stellar gridwork to the soul infused gridworks of the DE1D3s.

The second step was the join the thymus chakra and heart vortex fuelling the extra-stellar reality field with the vibrational level of the DE1D3 along with the integrated genetics.

And the third step was to increase the radiation energies, which would unfold when the hara quadrant had repaired and regenerated the two other vortexes as well as the integrated genetics and TEGs. The adding of the radiation energies happened through the combined throat chakra/throat vortex, activating the upper triangle with the elevated light coding enabling the genetics of the upper template to descend into the LPUHES.

The problems of DE2 and DE3 genetics and their less-progressive gridworks (not the dark areas) seemed solved and the ancient stellar races thrived along with the HMDE3s in the colonies.

The Rehabilitation Program
During the middle period of the colonies, the higher leveled LPRF3 reptoid races that had separated along with the soul races from the holographic metaverse or had left the HM to become part of the

Maldakian settlements, suffered a great deal from the post-timeline changes that had arisen from the timeline event. Most of the reptoid races from the LPRF3 Maldakian settlements were either extinct, had turned into dark ones or had escaped the timeline event by luck and had now become part of the post-timeline event settlements with the lesser evolved reptoid races, who had got their own area after the division of the two verses in the lower areas of the LPU. Here the more intelligent LPRF3 reptoids became their leaders and elders.[39]

The DE2D5 reptoid areas had undergone a solidification, which led to a denser organic body, than they were accustomed to. Some of the genetics, the DE2D5 reptoids had worked their way through in earlier elevation cycles, began to resurface with traits of insectoid, avian and reptilian behavior as well as adding the ancient animal features to the new organic form.

Most of the reptoids had had a humanlike appearance for ages and now the ancient animal features suddenly re-appeared in their organic make-up. This troubled them a lot; that is to see their humanlike features change into long past stages of reptilian, avian and insectoid features, which had only been part of their energy systems as integrated genetics, containing the memories of the previous cycles. The ancient stages of the primitive animal form of the fourth evolutionary cycle had not been seen for a long time, since most of the reptoids had already entered the mammal evolution or the pre-stages, which would lead them safely through the fourth elevation cycle.

The malfunction of the DE2D5 genetics, combined with the lack of soul genetics, changed their consciousness into a whole new type of alteration, creating a more primitive consciousness and they became highly violent. However since the regression had its cause in the

---

[39] The Maldakian reptoids were the highest evolved of the reptoid races, making them able to take part of the LPRF3 areas.

genetic malfunction because of the merged-in TEGs of the second generation, and not a breaking down, solutions could be found to bring the regression process to a halt. The elders, i.e. the preceding LPRF3 reptoids, turned to the colonies for help. Nonetheless the help came a bit too late, since sub-fields of the DE2D5 reptoid areas had already turned into *regression fields*[40] inhabited with the reptoids holding malfunctioning genetics and merged-in TEGs, where whole new races unfolded with scaly skin, wings and all sorts of insectoid, avian and reptilian features of which the winged reptilians, the later called draco-reptilians, became the leaders of the new areas since they were the largest, the most violent and held the highest level of the reptoid genetics. In other words, the draco-reptilians were the strongest and most intelligent of the regression field races.

From the regression fields the new insectoid-avian-reptoid races began to take over other areas of the DE2D5 by violent, hostile and intrusive methods unknown to the LPU and the HM. As the subfields had been taken over and the malfunctioning genetics were blended into the other reptoid settlers there, whole areas of the 5th dimension began to regress and along with this large sections of the gridwork of the DE2D5.

To ensure that the regressed insectoid-avian-reptoids did not take over additional sub-fields by performing horizontal merging of the malfunctioning genetics with the remaining reptoid settlers in the non-regressed areas, unprecedented technologies were invented to modify gridworks and genetics by the use of *vibrational scattering*, *dimensional splitting* and *genetic modification*. The technologies were intended to secure the higher levels of the 5th dimension from being

---

[40] The regression fields houses humanoids with malfunctioning genetics and merged-in TEGs, not infected as such, but regressing due to the changes of the light coding in the gridworks. They differ from the dark areas, because the dark areas arise from the infection.

fused with the malfunctioning genetics from the regression fields and their hostile races, by the use of modification of the reptoid genetics (integration of a *third generation of TEGs*) as well as isolating the regressed sub-fields of the 5th dimension by frequency scattering and dimensional split. The frequency scattering could hold back the regression process by scattering the regressed gridworks in its early stages, whereas the dimensional split could separate areas with fully regressed gridworks from the areas with non-regressed gridworks.

After the separation of the DE2D5s and the regressed insectoid-avian-reptoid races, the rehabilitation program was initiated as an attempt to heal the reptoids only having a small degree of regression.

In the rehabilitation program a non-regressed reptoid-mammal voluntarily projected his or her consciousness into the LPUHES of a regressed insectoid-avian-reptoid humanoid and by this the correctly working genetics of the non-regressed reptoid-mammal humanoid, who only projected his or her consciousness and by this kept his or her original LPUHES intact, would teach, adjust and re-align the malfunctioning genetics back on track.

The combined regressed and projected genetics were inserted into the restoration program DE1D3 energy system as an experiment to see if it was possible to reverse the regressed genetics this way. It was only done in a very few cases given the fact that most of the double energy systems did not work properly and internal counteracting behavior was the result, i.e. the genetics sort of created two sub-personalities of which one level of the energy system was ruled by the malfunctioning genetics and the other level by the non-regressed genetics, creating a sort of split personality.

Nevertheless, this program laid the foundation of the methods used to generate the ego of the chakra system in the technologies used by the dark ones later on.

The Reptilian Riots

Some of the draco-reptilian races of the regression fields rose to become leaders and took on the title as the overlords. Lesser clever draco-reptilians became the warriors or minions under the overlords.

The overlords unfolded a plan to leave the regression fields and cross the gap of their prison. Most of the regressed races joined them and they managed, by skillfully genetic engineering, to generate a sort of light coding shell around the malfunctioning strands of the genetics, giving them the appearance of being non-regressed, and by this enabling them to cross the gap into the non-regressed DE2D5 gridworks, who recognized the sealed-in genetics as reptoid.

The interdimensional gap, as with all dimensional sectors, was upheld by genetic recognition. After the draco-reptilians and their followers had crossed the gap, leaving some of the insectoid-avian-reptoid races behind since they had too high a level of regression (the ones left behind had literally turned into animals and had very little resemblance to any form of humanoid consciousness) the draco-reptilian overlords, the warriors and minions raided and revenged among the other reptoid races of the DE2D5 taking over most of the non-regressed DE2D5 systems as well as quite a huge chunk of the DE2D4 avian settlements. From the DE2D4 areas, the overlords and their insectoid-avian-reptoid minions entered the colonies. The three programs, along with the colonies, were taken over. All technologies invented to these programs were altered and turned into means of captivity of the colonial inhabitants who had not got out in time by separating their LPUHES from the DE1D3 energy system and returned home. The HMDE3s and the DE1D3 humanoids, which were not slain, retracted into hiding by lifting their genetics, energy systems and by this their organic form into a higher vibrational mode. All remaining humanoids from other systems were captured during the takeover or *the Reptilian Riots* as they later were called.

The Self-Healing Program

During the Reptilian Riots, before the full hijacking of the colonies, the HMDE3s and the DE1D3 humanoids could see where things were going in the other systems. They thus began the preparations for their future lives in Hallow Earth, as the DE2D4 and DE2D5 areas fell around them and were put under the control of the draco-reptilian overlords. Some of the DE1D3s chose to stay behind a bit longer than the rest, who actually retraced very early with the HMDE3s,[41] to ensure that a self-healing holographic program was completed and installed in the front areas of the bridge zones, which for the safety of the soul races, had been sealed off.

The self-healing holographic program (the SHHP), which was an interactive teaching system, would be ready to activate whenever someone held the correct ratio of soul genetics and TEGs or the third type of genetics in the DE1D3s. The SHHP would be activated, not by locality, but by genetic recognition of soul genetics or the third type of genetics and when activated, the SHHP would play a set of recordings of how to reactivate the soul genetics, reconnect to the DE1D3s or how to return to the HM through the bridge zones. If the genetics were correct, the SHHP would connect telepathically to the DE1D3s of Hallow Earth, get the soul genetics ready to grow the third type of genetics and by this, turn into a DE1D3 true earth humanoid to unfold when the draco-reptilian era was over. The bridge zones

---

[41] One of the abilities of the DE1D3 humanoids is to see into the future by monitoring the quanta of the timelines in a reality field and by this the manifestation rate of a gridwork. All timelines pointed in the direction of an era under the draco-reptilians.

front areas were not placed in time and space, but were linked up to the genetics of the upper template, when these were activated by the radiation energies. Therefore only humanoids, who had reached a higher level of restoration of the genetics resembling the soul genetic level of the HM, would be able to activate the SHHP. The DE1D3s hid the coding of the holographic interactive teaching system inside their genetics and energy systems. They deliberately did this because, at that time, rescue was fruitless for them given that the SHHP took longer time to generate than anticipated.

The DE1D3s that stayed behind to ensure the SHHP was available to the much later races of DE1D3s[42] were captured by the draco-reptilian factions. Many were slaughtered and genetically fragmented in blind revenge by the same technology that had separated the regressed races from the DE2D5 areas. The fragmented genetics from the remaining DE1D3 humanoids were then gathered and put into genetic programs generating new genetics or TEGs. Because of that the coding of the SHHP are hidden inside the genetics and TEGs being traded from this reality field to the other stellar races under the draco-reptilian supremacy, having used the different programs of the DE1D3s for their own purposes.

Others were separated from their quantum morphogenetic field, and by this pulled out of the DE1D3 humanoid form, and left as energy systems only holding genetics, with their personalities sealed off in the upper triangle. The sealed off energy systems with the third type of genetics were stored in hibernation chambers linked directly to the DE1D3 gridworks with the purpose of fuelling them, i.e. keeping the self-healing properties of the DE1D3 reality field intact. The coding is thus hidden in the DE1D3 gridworks as well through the hibernated DE1D3 energy systems, only awaiting their re-activation

---

[42] They knew that the draco-reptilian area would last for more than 26.000 years.

when they are awakened, which they will be at the end of the draco-reptilian era or through the resetting of the DE1D3 reality field.

Other Effects of the Riots

During the Reptilian Riots under the leadership of the draco-reptilian overlords most of the dimensional bridges were hijacked and divided among the regressed races as points of control of the DE1D3. The handing out of dimensional bridges was part of a fragile peace treaty between the draco-reptilian overlords and the other races having collaborated with them.

Other regressive races did not take part in the draco-reptilian alliances, such as the DE2D5 Orion Collective of avian-reptoid lizards (the scavengers). Instead they raided and took over areas of the 4th, 5th and the lower areas of the 6th dimensions (by the use of TEGs) and created various forms of prison fields to sustain and fuel their home systems with genetics, light coding and other supplies.

The DE2D5 avian-reptoid lizard landowners of the DE1D3 (more on this later on) were instated by the draco-reptilian overlords because of their political, economical and scientific abilities for growth and innovation, whereas the lesser advanced scavengers took what they wanted in the areas, where the draco-reptilian overlords had little or none interest. Hence, most of the systems outside the interest of the draco-reptilian overlords were left to the Orion Collective and turned into prison systems or left on their own, bleeding and destroyed. Not many of the systems left on their own rose back up on their feet and have from the Riots and on, undergone various changes.

Some systems have continued the regression of the genetics and are solely inhabited by animals. These animals were ancient stellar races to begin with but regressed back into their animal state. Without any infusion of the third generation of TEGs, the regression continued and these wilderness systems now only hold animal and plant lifeforms, leaving the remnants of the earlier highly developed stellar communities to decay and rot. Some of the animals from these systems have been imported to the DE1D3 reality field to become part of the DE1D3 genetic experimentation and growth of TEGs.

Changes within the DE1D3 Reality Field

The regressive DE2D5 and DE2D4 insectoid-avian-reptoid races under the draco-reptilian overlords had now taken over the most of the DE2D5, the DE2D4 and the DE1D3 reality fields and the captivators were in full process of creating a societal structure that would fit the economic and technological structure of their wishes. When I say economic, I am not talking about money but about the mechanisms of trade, which the regressive races had developed, by exchanging knowledge and genetics to support growth and substitution of light coding and TEGs. The exchange of light coding and TEGs made the regressive reality fields grow into new reality fields, unfolding new features based upon the upgrading of the regressed genetics. As such the whole DE2D5 and below had regressed into a crossing between the minor third elevation cycle and the passed fourth evolutionary cycle. The lower levels of the LPU had taken a turn back in evolution and yet unfolded new features of commerce, exchange of light coding etc. However the post-riot reality fields were based upon primitive behavior stemming from the regressed animal genetics, and not from the higher developed first generations of TEGs and LPU genetics from before the timeline event. The whole lower level of the LPU changed with the Reptilian Riots and the few remaining ancient stellar races retracted to the DE3 areas, which were linked up to the HM under the Sirian A lineages. The ones that did not manage to do this were captured, sealed off or slaughtered. Most of the ancient stellar races were eradicated throughout the Reptilian Riots and their genetics were fragmented and inserted into regressive energy systems. These fragments became the foundation for *the fourth generation of TEGs* and thus the basis of the new stellar races. Naturally the lineages of the DE2D6 reptoid-mammal Sirian Bs[43] have not been put into this equation and we also lack the dark ones, who will show up on the scene later on.

The DE1D3 system proved prosperous in terms of the production of new versions of TEGs and genetic cultivating. The draco-reptilian overlords held storages of the fragmented DE1D3 humanoid genetics as well as genetics from the ancient stellar races the draco-Reptilian had encountered, slaughtered or captured during their voyages of rioting throughout the DE1D3 and DE2 systems.

The template genetics from the slaughtered ancient stellar races where harvested by separating the upper template from the level one energy system (harsh technologies were used) and stored for later trade. Other captured stellar races from the DE2 and DE1D3 systems (including visiting DE3s and additional races) were sealed off leaving the level one energy system active and ready to be borrowed by visiting DE2 insectoid-avian-reptoid races from the systems under the draco-reptilian overlords. Many of the visiting DE2 stellar races had no time or did not want to unfold a DE1D3 organic form and thus needed a travelling suit for their work here.[44]

The draco-reptilian overlords have kept the genetics along with the hibernated ancient stellar races in secure areas and here they have developed, through the use of lizard and insectoid minions, new

---

[43] Which covers the Shiva-Aryans, the crystalline Sirian Bs, the remaining Maldakian lineages and most of the reptoid-mammal Pleiadian and Arcturian races; i.e. most of the stellar races having a human-like appearance.

[44] Projection of another personality, from a different dimensional humanoid, into the stored level one energy system (the LPUHES), where the upper triangle is sealed off and thus inactive, has been used a lot in our reality field. Indeed to such an extent that many of the LPUHES have now reached such a level of decay that the genetics inside the LPUHES are burned out. If this happens, the upper template will separate and the genetics in it can be harvested and put into a new template, creating a whole new level one energy system.

fields of sciences of which most have been sold to the insectoid-avian-reptoid races longing for an upgrade of their genetics back to the level they had before the regression.

To control the prosperous DE1D3 areas, because of the healing gridworks, DE2D5 humanoids holding avian-reptoid genetics, called the lizards landowners (the bloodlines of the nobilities), were instated directly into the DE1D3 areas to control the trade and to ensure that the property of the draco-reptilian overlords grew in value. DE2D4 avian-mammal humanoids (avian genetics with mammal TEGs) were instated to function as mediators between the races living in the DE1D3 reality field, i.e. modified, captured humanoids from other systems and the avian-reptoid lizard landowners plus connecting to the DE2D5 draco-reptilian overlords when this was needed. The avian-mammal races also controlled who came in and who could rent an energy suit to sojourn the DE1D3 areas.

In the hierarchy of power, the DE2D4 avian-mammal humanoids were answering to the DE2D5 avian-reptoid landowners, who were the ones holding the true power of the DE1D3, answering directly to the draco-reptilian overlords. The DE2D4 avian-mammal races mostly functioned as priests for the DE2D5 landowners and did their bidding. The main work was as magicians performing different types of energy work, mostly with the intent of harming other landowners, or to create portals enabling the lizards to communicate with the draco-reptilian overlords and so forth.[45]

The Rise of the Two Brotherhoods
The first undivided brotherhood rose out of the DE2D4 priestly avian-mammal races of which we know two segments: the Annunaki, i.e. the Mesopotamia-African-Mediterranean segment and the Avestian

---

[45] In religion priests are the link between the unknown and not-worthy humans and the "gods". All religions are invented by the priestly DE2D4 avian-mammal brothers.

faction, i.e. the Iran-India-Mongolian segment. The Avestian faction did not arise before around 1700-1300 BCE and their lineage differs from the Annunaki faction, which is seen in the slightly different type of religion of the areas, they have lived in.[46] On the other hand the Annunaki, i.e. the Mesopotamia-African-Mediterranean DE2D4 avian-mammal races, are older and they are depicted in Mesopotamian art showing the Assyrian Tree of Life with the landowners or kings from a avian-reptoid lineage and the bird-headed avian-mammal priests (the Annunaki) standing behind them, ensuring the kings their power, the connection to the gods (the draco-reptilian overlords) as well as securing a portal out of the DE1D3 reality field, when needed (after death).[47]

The winged Sun of Thebes depicts upper and lower Egypt seen in the headpieces of the snakes.[48]

We see the winged sun in Egyptian, Assyrian, Babylonian and Jewish (Judah) art.[49] The winged sun is a symbol of royalty and divinity. It is also the symbol for the old factions of the brotherhood of priests and their kings, i.e. *the Old World Order* (the OWO).

The two snakes on under the Egyptian winged sun symbolize the upper and lower kingdoms of ancient Egypt under the semi-feudal rulers acting as provincial governors of the 42 nomes of Egypt. The

---

[46] The religion of Zarathustra is an example stemming from around 1600-1300 BCE. Many religions are influenced by the Zarathustra beliefsystem; i.e. the idea of demons (deavas) and angels (ahuras) stem from this beliefsystem. The asuras and devas are also seen in the Rig Vedas, which stem from the same segment around the same time period (1700-1100 BCE).

[47] Search for the Assyrian Tree of Life, British Museum or go to the link below
https://mesocosm.files.wordpress.com/2011/12/img_5998.jpg

[48] Find *Egyptian Mythology and Egyptian Christianity* by Samuel Sharpe, 1863 on
https://archive.org/details/egyptianmytholog00shar

[49] See http://en.wikipedia.org/wiki/Winged_sun

governors[50] held diverse types of avian-reptoid genetics and they came from the DE2D4-DE2D5 collaborative areas under the draco-reptilian overlords. Upper and lower Egypt were united around 3000 BCE, however the division of Egypt into nomes lasted up until the Roman period,[51] where the Roman Empire continued the division of the land between the nobilities and the ones in power.[52]

Before the fusion of upper and lower Egypt around 3000 BCE, perhaps under King Scorpio II[53] or Narmer[54], the Egyptians were under the influence from Mesopotamia cf. the avian priestly races controlling this area as well. In ancient times the world, from South America to Africa to the Mediterranean, from Mesopotamia to India and up to Mongolia, was under full protectorate of the draco-reptilian overlords, the lizards and the brotherhood. The ancient world, covering the middle DE1D3 areas, was the place of interstellar trade, collaboration and exchange of goods, not only as gold and minerals, but also as genetics. In this period the dimensional bridges (stargates) were still working, creating bridges of travel to all of the other reality fields of the regressed parts of the LPU.

All interstellar races could enter and leave the ancient world if they had agreements with the draco-reptilian overlords. This period is the Atlantean era,[55] including the ancient stellar colonies, and it extends from around 250,000 years ago until around 12,500 years ago. The brotherhood was founded during the later stages of the Atlantean era. The undivided brotherhood later had a huge trial in the

---

[50] Called Nomarchs: http://en.wikipedia.org/wiki/Nomarch
[51] http://en.wikipedia.org/wiki/Upper_and_Lower_Egypt
[52] Historically the Roman Laws extend back to the lizard landowners.
[53] http://en.wikipedia.org/wiki/King_Scorpion
[54] http://en.wikipedia.org/wiki/Narmer
[55] This is the true Atlantis and not the stories of Plato, holding astral glamour. Most humans today confuse visions from other reality fields with the archetype of Atlantis. The archetype of Atlantis is a sub-program of the astral barrier, preventing us from reaching back to our stellar consciousness.

main council of the brotherhood around 26,000 years ago in what we know as Egypt, where the brotherhood ended up dividing over matters of whether they should continue to support the draco-reptilian overlords and lizards (the controllers for short), without questioning their actions, or if they should attempt to re-connect to the Maia-Pleiadians and Sirian As, of which some of the brothers had got in contact, learning the true history of the DE1D3 areas and not the stories that developed during the draco-reptilian reign. The false stories were developed to support the superiority of the overlords as the highest evolved races, and thus they were entitled to the elite rights to control all of the DE2D5, the DE2D4 and the DE1D3 systems.

The trial divided the brotherhood into two sections; the right wing (the RWBs) and the left wing (the LWBs). The right wing wished to evolve the DE1D3s back into its original progression scheme of the Maia-Pleiadians and Sirian As, whereas the left wing only wanted to keep things as they were, as in keeping things under the control of the draco-reptilian overlords. That is at least until the dark ones came messing up the division of the two brotherhoods, complicating things.

How to Recognize the Old World Order
Religious and political beliefsystems to govern *the societal structure* are part of the OWO. In the old days religion and political power were linked together. In modern day world religion and politics have been divided in most countries. Today New Age has taken the place of a united religion, being the updated version of the ancient religions, trying to combine all religious systems into one main religious system as attempted during the reign of Alexander.

The OWO religions entail:
- Visions of good and bad forces, helping or counteracting your effort in life.

- Belief in a higher power that guides you.
- Belief in that you are less worthy than the gods, the forces assisting you and the supreme power.
- You have travelled here because you wanted to take part of this planet of "suffering" to learn something that you lack in your soul make-up. To become a better soul!
- Belief in that you are here to learn because you have sinned, been badly, have karma, have fallen from higher dimensions and similar explanations why you are forced to be here. You are here because you deserve it!

Political systems are based upon a united nation, Europe and similar collaboration where the power is centralized in few ruling organs, either as one leader or any type of "democracy" unfolding the power of the chosen ones, all holding the correct bloodline. Not that the politicians are aware of this, usually not, but the minds of the politicians are able to be overshadowed by the personality of a LWB, directing them by the use of "intuition" and "strong feelings pro- og against something". Politic ideas are seeded as well into these puppet humans.

The OWO political systems support:
- One ruler, one major party, one religion, one God.
- Pseudo-democracy with elections of the nobilities.
- Pseudo-freedom and free will systems.
- Different political parties all about how to rule the country, as if common man had something to say in this.
- Power and political systems are all based upon money and the right to take part in this system of rich and poor.

- Some humans are more worthy than others and for this reason the division of people into groups of those with power and those without are the order of nature.

Societal structures and laws are all based upon:
- Money and trade.
- Circulation and manufacturing of goods.
- Supply and demand.
- Rulers and subjects.
- Hierarchical systems having those with power and money and those without.
- Households resembling the Roman structure with the father as the Patron and leader.
- Patron-client systems; still working today in a more modern version.
- The Roman Law system pertain to present day law complex.[56]
- The Law still supports the one in power and with money.
- Higher or lesser degree of taking care of the lesser fortunate as a sign of power and wealth.

Humans are viewed as dispensable resources meant as producers of genetics to support other stellar races in need of a certain vibration as well as a thousand other experimental programs all supporting the adjacent stellar systems.

Most countries in Europe incl. Scandinavia, the Mediterranean, the Middle East, India, South America and Africa are still under the ruler ship of the Old World Order. The battles in Iraq, Syria and other places where US Military and Government meddle with the Old

---

[56] Look up Roman Maxims or visit: http://ecclesia.org/truth/maxims.html Look aside from the Christian input and focus on the Roman Laws.

World Order, with the official goal of instigating democracy etc. have to do with the battles between newer stellar races working through their human counterparts and the avian-mammal races and avian-reptoid races that came here first.

The political intrigues around the world are a result of the internal battles between the three factions of the brotherhoods, i.e. the dark ones, the LWBs and RWBs where humans are used as means to fight the endless warring amongst these races, over the control of the DE1D3 reality field.

The Rise of the Dark Brothers

Just as some of the right wing brothers (the RWBs) had discovered the Maia-Pleiadian and Sirian A races, a minor faction of the left wing brothers (the LWBs) began co-working with the distorted LPRF3s from the dark areas (the dark zones of the DE3). As the RWBs had begun questioning the power of the draco-reptilian overlords, so did this faction, but not with the goal of assisting the captured and utilized ancient stellar races and others like them, but to gain power. This faction of the LWBs wanted to take over the DE1D3 areas and regain control over their DE2D4 home systems.

For this they coupled up with the dark LPRF3s, who had a wish to leave the dark areas. The dark LPRFs, i.e. the dark ones, were in dire need of supplementing genetics to stay alive (nearly everyone of the early infected humanoids had dissolved) and since most of remaining dark ones came from the Sirian workstations, they had a stronger grid in their energy system, making them able to uphold energy to keep them alive. On top of this the dark ones were highly intelligent and innovative and they offered solutions to the LWBs of how to turn the power of the draco-reptilian overlords around. The connection came through what we call dark magic (meaning that it links up to the dark antagonistic core and the dark ones) and happened accidently one day when one of the LWBs did his service for a landowner. Due to his high level of hate, anger and resentment, plus a dash of TEGs starting to break down, the energy work performed a loop and jumped into the dark areas instead of connecting to the DE2D5 overlord, seeking the same level of light coding that was instigated by the LWB in the energy work.

After this he continued the communication with the dark ones and eventually got a whole faction of the LWBs to join him in this effort. This first LWB is to this day the hierophant of the dark faction of the LWBs. This faction of the LWBs founded the dark brotherhood and as the dark ones crossed the gap between the dark areas and fused with the LWB energy systems of the dark faction, by adding dark TEGs[57], the dark masters of our reality field arose.

From the DE1D3 dark brotherhood (all inclusive) the dark ones set their mind to control portions of the DE2 and through communication portals and persuasion done by the dark LWBs, other regressive races became part of the dark LWBs entering the DE1D3 reality field on the new terms. These DE2 possessed regressive races hosting a dark one, took over the science labs, the genetics programs and the technology that had been set up under the draco-reptilian reign. They took over by a subtle invasion done from within possessing the ones working inside the science labs, programs and similar programs: following the possessing the workers turned dark and literally became hosts of a dark one or held a projecting dark LWB.[58]

New programs and sciences were invented to support the genetic supplements of the dark ones, and slowly the dark LWBs won the position within the rest of the LWB, as the supreme rulers. Many

---

[57] Dark TEGs are invented by the integrated dark ones and enable the dark ones to stay inside the avian-mammal body, i.e. their LWB host.
[58] Possession is done by projection of consciousness or by horizontal/vertical integration of genetics into the level one energy system.

things happened during the period from 12,500 BCE where the OWO, i.e. the draco-reptilian overlords, the avian-reptoid lizards and the avian-mammal priestly races shifted from being the authority of the DE1D3 systems and up until around 3500 BCE, where the LWBs and the dark faction finally had found a common footstool in how to control and rein this reality field.

The OWO structure with the kingdoms ruled by different lizard landowners, their intermediary priests under the draco-reptilian overlords remained and the OWO controlled the middle DE1D3 areas as in the economical and societal structure, whereas the dark ones got a portion of the encapsulated and sealed off energy systems, either won by persuasion of power or handed over in trade of dark separation technology to the rest of the LWBs under the draco-reptilian overlords.

However the total control over the ancient world only lasted until around 3000 BCE where other DE2D5 stellar races began entering the scene and claiming their share of the DE1D3 and the genetics stored there. They wanted part of the programs and some joined either the draco-reptilian factions, the LWBs under the dark ones or the RWBs, while others took over areas of the ancient world in a direct takeover. Many of the dimensional bridges were destroyed under the attempts to take the power away from the draco-reptilian overlords. The draco-reptilian overlords were slowly but surely losing their sovereign position. However the DE2D4 and DE2D5 areas bridging to the outer DE1D3 areas and most of the middle DE1D3 areas remained under the LWBs and the draco-reptilian overlords (the OWO).

Thus, as the middle and late dynasties were formed in Egypt a new faction of DE2D5 reptoid-mammal humanoids had taken over the control of Egypt and the rest of Africa (an alliance between what we understand as the Nordics and the Pleiadians) and these races gave power to the Pharaoh. The shift of power in Egypt forced the draco-reptilians, the lizards and the LWBs to focus their attention from the old areas of trade and wealth into new areas, today known as Europe. To begin the new era of dominion, they instigated a renewed attempt of one united world under the OWOs, generating the new political systems under Alexander the great around 323 BCE, where Egypt once more came under the footstool of the LWBs.

From the time when the dark ones entered, the lizards and the priestly LWBs had not gotten along well, since the avian-reptoids (the lizards) felt that the avian-mammal races (the LWBs) had abandoned the overlords, which they as such had.

The LWBs were diplomatically playing along with both the dark ones as well as the draco-reptilian overlords, satisfying the demands of both groups, and in this dubious game they had gained a new level of power, which threatened the position of the avian-reptoids. Internal conflicts were fought between the lizard rulers and the priestly LWBs, where the draco-reptilian overlords paired up with the lizards of whom they shared a genetic lineage rather than the genetic dissimilarity of avian-mammal LWBs. The kingdoms that ruled the late Mesopotamia and Mediterranean including the Roman Empire, their rise and down fall all bear witness to the conflicts between the avian-mammal LWBs and the draco-reptilian overlords and their lizard affiliates. These internal conflicts prevail to this day.

The Reign of the Dark Ones

As we get closer to our own type of reality, things get more dark and complicated. In the old days the DE2 ancient stellar races took part of the DE1D3 reality field and lived in the settings whether it was during the ancient stellar colonies or the later ancient world order under the lizards and the priestly races.

However after the LWB faction had begun their collaboration with the dark ones, the light coding was altered further in specific areas of the DE1D3 reality field to fit the agenda of the dark masters and the dark LWB brothers. As the draco-reptilian overlords had lost their sovereignty, the lizards and the LWBs fought over the remnants of the ancient world, while other DE2D5 stellar races gained power over specific areas of the ancient world. During all of these internal battles the dark LWBs succeeded in generating the blueprint for a buffer zone that would seal off the core and middle areas of the DE1D3 as well as cutting off the dimensional bridges to DE2 systems under the Sirian A lineages and the bridge zones to the holographic metaverse.

The blueprint of the circular buffer zone was generated by magical endeavors making a portion of the holographic DE1D3 light coding reverse even further and by this counteracting the bridging zones as well as separating the encircled area from the rest of the DE1D3 reality field, minimizing our solar system into what it is today.

For the dark LWBs and their allies the goal was to generate an enclosure that would feed the dark ones with the needed genetics to sustain their dissolving energy systems. The LWBs worshipped their dark masters and they were infused with the infected genetics in their contact with them, voluntarily in rituals. Most of the rituals were performed to gain access to the antagonistic dark core and with it creating portals between the DE1D3 to the dark DE3s, having the dark LWBs as hosts or carriers of the dark TEGs.

The history is, as we have learned, that the dark DE3 areas had been sealed off by the ancient stellar races after the timeline event, and that one LWB managed to break the seals and reconnect to the dark ones.

The dark ones were constantly in the process of seizing to exist and were supposed to stop existing – that was the whole goal of the sealing off – but in contact with living genetics their dissolving energy systems could function a bit longer and with it activate the dangerous infection into the humanoids they came in contact with.

Their energy systems were stuck in the sealed off dark areas[59] but their consciousness could extend beyond that and into the minds and energy systems of the minions collaborating with them, acting as hosts in the other dimensions. But the dark ones did not need all the other DE2 areas to thrive off, they only needed one highly energetic and diverse reality field, where as much as possible genetics were gathered and easy to take over. The DE1D3 was the answer to this search due to the ancient stellar colonies and the many forms of programs that had developed from these, holding stored up genetics or grown as it had become a tendency among the regressed stellar races under the draco-reptilian overlords, working inside the DE1D3 reality field.

The Rise of the Enclosure

The dark ones and their minions had been an active factor since the 2500 BCE where they instigated the foundation of the enclosure but it

---

[59] Whether or not there is some sort of form in the DE3 dark zones is an open question. The dark ones usually work through another organic form having possessed this or through an astral form.

was not until the dark middle ages that the barrier came into its full manifestation, sealing off the middle and core areas of the DE1D3 from the rest of the DE2 new stellar races, existing in the outskirts of the DE1D3 connected to the DE2D4 and DE2D5 systems. Historians today say that the dark middle ages were not as dark as hitherto acknowledged in terms of cultural creations and enlightened thinking; nevertheless for me the dark middle ages have nothing to do with cultural settings, albeit all to do with the darkening of the light coding of the core and middle areas of the DE1D3,[60] which around the year 1548 had sunk into the darkest state in the history of the DE1D3. And why is that?

During the 1100's the dark ones managed to possess more and more of their minions inside the middle areas of the DE1D3 reality field making the blueprint of the barrier and the sub-programs to uphold it stronger. Instead of only working through the dark LWBs, now functioning among the padres of the Catholic Church,[61] they realized that they could go further and gain more power.

The dark LWBs had always performed the needed rituals to secure the required genetics to their masters by offering powers, security or other things to the RWB brothers or other LWBs of the non-dark factions in exchange for their genetics. The OWO (including the LWB, the RWB and the lizards) administered the daily life inside the middle DE1D3 areas as a joint effort to secure the highest outcome of the sealed off energy systems etc along with the different regressive DE2 stellar races present in the middle and outer DE1D3 areas from the various reality fields, collaborating to get as much out of the DE1D3 as possible. The good intentions of the ancient stellar races that

---

[60] Go to the chapter on *The Dimensional Bridges* to understand the core, middle and outer areas of the DE1D3.

[61] This took place before the Lutheran priests came into existence. Then there were dark LWBs among them too.

created the restoration and regeneration programs thousands of years earlier were long gone and the newer generations had taken over the DE1D3 labs, scientific programs and technology altered it all into their conveniences. Given that these purposes were more self-centered and less altruistic than the predecessors, the dark ones and their dark priests had no problem in finding willing victims to fit their scheme of sustaining the hunger of the dark ones with promises of gaining power or solving life threatening issues.[62]

The dark ones decided to go even further and take over the DE1D3 core and middle areas in full. Having taking out many of the RWBs by dark separation technology, and influencing stakeholders, leaders and other leading characters of the OWO from around 2500 BCE and up to the year 1548, the dark ones managed to take over more and more of the power from the new generations of the regressed stellar races, pushing them out or making them leave by choice.

While the dark ones gained more power, their dark genetics began affecting the gridworks of the core and middle areas of the DE1D3, creating distortions in the self-healing mechanisms of the gridworks. As a result the other regressed stellar races pulled out and back to the secure DE2D4 or DE2D5 areas, leaving the DE1D3 unattended and ready to be taken over. The only stellar races left inside the middle areas of the DE1D3 were the encapsulated and sealed off ancient stellar races, now functioning as the sustaining principle of the middle area organic form, some of the LWBs and RWBs as well as the lizard landowners having adjusted to the settings of the middle areas of the DE1D3s. The lizards had survived by breeding into chosen lineages

---

[62] I have several chakra mappings of RWBs that give away some of their genetics in the template to the dark ones to solve situations involving children or spouses suffering from illness or having been infected with the dark genetics. The dark LWBs would then "sell" the solution to the RWBs which, at that point in time, had detached themselves from the Sirian A races and therefore were controlled by fear or by greed, wanting to gain more power.

holding a specific kind of bio-genetics, which led to organic bodies that could hold and express their level one energy system, integrated DE2D5 avian-reptoid genetics and stellar personality. As the RWBs were taken over by their greed or fear, buying into the dark LWB agenda, the protective faction of the encapsulated and sealed off energy systems of the ancient stellar races seized to exist and the dark and their affiliated LWBs gained the full control over the hibernated or inserted ancient stellar energy systems. This came to a completion around 1548.

During the 1600´s clones were created of the viable level one energy systems and a large program to produce more human bodies (the middle area organic form) from these clones, were activated and set in motion with the intention of doubling the organic forms.

For the dark ones the middle area organic form and its level one energy system became the perfect vehicle to produce whatever they needed of energy and viable genetics. The dark ones and the dark LWBs as well as the rest of the LWBs accepting their new masters as a fact, generated a new infrastructure of the DE1D3 middle areas, i.e. our present reality.

We still see a few visits in the middle ages from the other stellar races but the visits dried out as the core and middle DE1D3 field were taken over by dark ones. It became a highly risky place to visit and only few races did after the year 1548, where the middle DE1D3[63] fell under the distorted energies of the dark ones. The middle DE1D3 had been turned into the worst type of prison field ever seen in this quadrant.

Yes, the scavengers had their prison fields, running these fields as huge mining operations and similar facilities to support their home systems with the various substances that could only be produced in

---

[63] The middle areas of the DE1D3s cover the perimeter from the Moon to Mars. Venus and Jupiter are the beginning of the outer areas of the DE1D3.

the prison fields because of the unique genetic set up of the races living there, or the light coding of the gridworks.

Nevertheless, the prison fields were inhabited by aware regressed humanoids, knowing their destiny and what was going on although many of the prison fields developed habits and customs that for most of the other regressed stellar races seemed barbaric and totally off the chart of what was considered normal behavior.

Since the core and middle areas of the DE1D3 were already set up to grow a variety of genetics – the other reality fields could only grow one type according to the races living there and the DE1D3 could grow all of the genetics of the DE2 reality fields – the encapsulated races inside of the middle areas of the DE1D3 changed from being the providers of genetics to the regressed stellar races into becoming the main genetic suppliers for the dark ones after the full take over.

Naturally most of the genetic programs were still running under the remaining DE2D5 lizards and the non-dark LWBs, who had made several prosperous deals with the dark ones in spite of the takeover.

All RWBs inside the core and middle DE1D3 areas were captured and sealed off. Present regressive stellar races that did not get out, or accepted the new terms by trickery, underwent the same procedure. All organic forms were rounded up and changed to fit the further reversed light coding of core and middle DE1D3 areas, having been altered extra by the meddling with the 12 crystal pillars upholding the core and middle DE1D3 areas.

The healing abilities of DE1D3 energy system were laid dormant, as well as the pineal and pituitary glands, sealing off the ability to reconnect to the level one energy system on a conscious level. The level one energy systems were sealed off in all DE1D3 forms present in the enclosure and only the five lower chakras of the organic form were left functional to keep the body together. Obviously the lizards and LWBs had their progression chakras intact (the hara quadrant) in the organic form and by this functioning through their level one energy system, its template and the genetics. The genetics were mostly regressed genetics; however a few held the old versions of the TEGs and were therefore still able to progress out of the DE1D3.

The middle DE1D3 area humanoids and all other present stellar races were then linked up to distortion technologies placed in the core areas of the DE1D3 manipulating the 12 crystal pillars to produce further reversed light coding,[64] altering the progression fields of the DE1D3 energy system. Then a central chakra, the solar plexus chakra, was added to control the hara quadrant (the progression abilities of the chakra system) pulling away the incoming light coding from the throat, heart and root chakras and their connected vortexes, and instead circulating the incoming energies into the hara chakra and solar plexus chakra, generating a whole new type of earth human. By this the level one energy system, along with the seals, were detached from the DE1D3 energy system.

The distortion technologies in the core changed the light coding of the DE1D3 middle areas into something entirely new, reversing the progression dynamics into steady state fields, where genetics could not progress further unless they were extracted from the level one energy system. The DE1D3 energy system was altered into the various functions we see today and the level one energy system was kept attached, not for progression, but to fuel the growth processes of the genetics inserted into the chakras for various purposes.

New trade systems were set up around the dark controlled DE1D3, using DE2 allied to hand over the genetics without getting in contact

---

[64] The LPU is founded on reversed light coding to keep it separated from the HM; however the dark technologies reversed the light coding even more to generate the enclosure. The further reversed light coding separate the core and middle DE1D3 areas from the outer DE1D3 areas and all of the other dimensions bordering into the DE1D3.

with the distorted DE1D3 areas. Raiding groups of scavengers found a new income in capturing and torturing stellar races in the adjacent reality fields surrounding the DE1D3, which were not under the dark ones. Innocent stellar humanoids were captured and stripped of their organic form, after which the energy system and the template were shipped into the DE1D3 enclosure where it was traded to the highest bidding of either a dark LWB, a king or a political leader in need of a new level one energy system since the old one, sustaining the organic form, was wearing out. Naturally the capturing of viable energy systems for trade was not a new thing; it had been part of the other races controlled by the draco-reptilians for eons to utilize their many genetic programs or to grant the visiting higher dimensional races a body in the DE1D3 systems. However the use of a sealed off level one energy systems by the dark ones added new levels to the trade of captured energy systems given that the dark ones quickly wore out the overtaken energy system since their infected genetics dissolved the integrated genetics in the process. Therefore the dark ones had to invent new technologies to follow up on the new levels of trade, not only to sustain their own energy systems, but also because the dark ones saw an opportunity to gain more power through the new trade and sciences.

When the integrated genetics in the energy system wear out, the template separates from the energy system. The template genetics can then be harvested, and inserted into a *similar* new energy system *for integration*, sustaining the other energy system or making it able to gain access to other dimensions. The template genetics have not been added with the personality traits of the upper triangle and are thus neutral, so to speak, only holding the possibilities, they were added when put into the template.

The harvested genetics can also be inserted into another energy system *for incubation*, as in placing the template genetics inside a

101

dissimilar level one energy system, which in turn will adapt and develop them. The level one energy systems chosen as incubators are sealed off accordingly to unfold this function and certain chakras are engineered and added to be able to process the genetic incubation. When the incubated genetics are mature, they will be pulled out and inserted into the energy system of either a dark one or a LWB, or some other stellar humanoid present here to do work but not having the time or interest in doing the hard developmental work with the genetics.

Without the template, the remaining integrated genetics in the level one energy system will fragment into bits and can be pulled out of the energy system as individual units encapsulated in light coding. They are then inserted into other DE1D3 energy systems, the chakras, with a specific purpose.

As the integrated genetics are separated from the energy system, the knowledge and memories of the personality are scattered along with the bits, generating the idea of the personality being incarnated in multiple human forms at once. In reality it is the scattered genetics inserted into multiple chakra systems, which continue to unfold the consciousness recording through the many bodies, they have been put into. The genetic bits remain interconnected with each other and continue to function as a whole, just like they did when they were part of the original level one energy system and personality. Since the bits are linked together, as in operating from the same consciousness platform, they communicate across time and space trying to regain the original whole or unity.

The search for unity is what pulls the bits in diverse directions and because of this they are excellent to put into the DE1D3 energy system (the chakra system) confusing the chakras. The diversion from the inserted fragmented genetics is a secondary security measure, enacted to ensure that the chakras cannot by accident activate the hara quadrant and reconnect to the sealed off level one energy system. Through these genetic programs and sciences the dark ones were now in control of the DE1D3 area and with it they began to expand into the reality fields linked up to the DE1D3 through the dimensional bridges. To secure that the dark ones would not spread further, the other DE2 races decided to quarantine the whole DE1D3 system, sealing in the imprisoned stellar races to an unknown destiny of utilization of their energy systems and genetics as nutrition for the dark ones.

The Astral Plane

As the dark ones and their infected allies, along with the LWB minions and similar avian-reptoid humanoid races took over the DE1D3 areas in this sector, the energies dropped significantly. The reality fields of the middle DE1D3 areas dropped to a 2.5 dimensional setting,[65] separating the middle DE1D3 areas from its 3rd dimensional quantum features, making the whole manifested reality turn rigid. The rigidity in the reality fields began accumulating the diversion energies of the fragmented bits in the chakra systems as well as the emission from the distortion technologies of the core.

The quarantine of the whole DE1D3 system added to the problem, which kept the DE1D3 reality fields in a closed feedback system, preventing new light coding to enter the gridworks. It did not help that the remaining stellar energy systems were sealed off and their energy fields changed into what we today call the aura. Without the infusion of light coding from other dimensions that could lead to progression, the chakra systems clogged and started to emit distorted light coding, which is called astral energies in other teachings. The astral energies grew and they gathered together around the core and

---

[65] Today the setting is 2.8 and rising. When the middle DE1D3 area reaches the normal 3rd dimensional settings, the resetting will be completed.

middle DE1D3 areas adding a new level of energy to the enclosure. Here they produced a new field of reality, called the astral plane or the astral barrier since these two things are the same.

As we know from the Rebuilding Earth videos, the astral plane ended up being the place of the reintegration fields from where the reincarnation cycles are performed.[66] The reintegration fields house the level one energy systems that are left to burn out, due to too small amounts of viable genetics and thus have been stripped of their template. The reintegration areas hold the cloned energy systems as well, which rose to new levels during the 1700-1800's, where the human population began to rise exponentially. The level one energy system inside the reintegration fields are put there because they are of no further use for the dark ones or the LWBs.[67]

---

[66] It here becomes difficult with the dating, because reincarnation as an idea has been part of the Indian teachings from around 6th century BCE. However the idea of reincarnation in the old texts does not mean the same thing as we understand it today. The present understanding of reincarnation and lives between lives are a late addition and is part of the 1548 enclosure. Earlier ideas of reincarnation is linked to the level one energy system, as Wikipedia write: "There is no word corresponding exactly to the English terms "rebirth", "metempsychosis", "transmigration" or "reincarnation" in the traditional languages of Pāli and Sanskrit. The entire universal process that gives rise to the cycle of death and rebirth, governed by karma, is referred to as Samsara, while the state one is born into, the individual process of being born or coming into the world in any way, is referred to simply as "birth" (jāti). Devas (gods) may also die and live again. Here the term "reincarnation" is not strictly applicable, yet Hindu gods are said to have reincarnated."
https://en.wikipedia.org/wiki/Reincarnation
Reincarnate means to take on organic form once more and thus do not refer as such to "a soul" being reincarnated, as we understand it today. The ancient Greek ideas of metamorphosis are not based upon the same ideas as reincarnation as we know it, but are linked to the stoic ideas of a cyclical cosmos repeating itself over and over. The Buddhist ideas are linked to the cycles of the skandhas and the eternal self, which is not a self as in an individual but a principle of Nirvana, which it returns to as purified consciousness.
http://www.trans4mind.com/personal_development/buddhist/5skandhas.htm
[67] The lizards have their own scientific systems of genetic reproduction and utilization and thus do not use the same techniques or methods as the LWBs.

104

Consequently the energy systems and integrated genetics are left to burn out in the astral plane. Here they create a new secondary personality from the many reincarnation cycles and the periods in between on the astral plane, given that the reintegration fields hold communities with schools etc.[68] The new personality is made out of astral energy, slightly added with the fragmented genetics, and it comes into being through the reincarnation cycles and the time spent on the astral plane.

The goal of the reincarnation is to get the integrated genetics ready to be harvested as bits. One day the level one energy system is fully burned out, and in time of death – shedding off the organic form at the end of the final incarnation – the burned out energy system does not return to the reintegration fields since it is led to the "mental areas" as fragmented bits.

The mental areas are science labs in the upper levels of the middle DE1D3 areas under the administration of the LWBs and to some degree the lizards who are present there, performing their scientific genetic programs or for the trade of genetic bits.

The upper levels of the middle DE1D3 areas exist outside the astral plane near the outer DE1D3 areas and thus connected to the stellar races living inside the outer DE1D3 area, i.e. the collaborating factions and allies of the LWBs or the lizards.

In spite of the quarantine the outer DE1D3 areas are still linked to the allied systems through the dimensional bridges but only because of later peace treaties done between the supreme councils of the rest of the DE2. The supreme councils of the DE2D5 are mostly under the draco-reptilian overlords, whereas the DE2D4 and DE2D6 supreme councils today are under the Sirian Bs.

---

[68] For further investigation of the lives in between lives and the afterlife read the books of Micheal Newton.

The Methods of Control of the Dark Ones

The dark ones have handed over the control of the societal structures beneath the astral barrier to the OWO and the LWBs, with whom they collaborate. The dark ones only interfere directly with individuals if they are of special interest. The dark ones thus only use methods of control if they are especially interested in a person holding genetics they want. Methods of control are also used if a person is seen as a threat to their dominion or if a person is part of the factions working against the dark ones. Sometimes the LWBs and the lizards utilize the dark methods of control as well.

The methods are:

- Stellar surveillance technology inside and outside the house.
- DE1D3 energy system control technologies reversed from the ancient colonial technologies that were created to assist the progress of the stellar races taking part in the programs.
- Magically affected implants (created of astral energies, the intention of the creator and sometimes stellar technology) inserted into the aura and DE1D3 energy system to control the energies here.
- Overshadowing of mind and emotions; steering them into good or lesser good directions, leading to actions based upon these thoughts and feelings.
- Astral (elemental) bugs that are sent into our homes affecting the energies to unfold vibrations amplifying our emotional and mental abilities in the way they want.
- Elemental bugs sent to affect thoughtforms; such as suicidal thinking, fearbased ideas, delusional thought patterns, etc.
- Energy symbols put into the aura, draining the aura and DE1D3 energy system of energy as well as instigating illness etc.

- Direct contact with the chosen ones, or the ones sent to assist you in your "special service" serving as the messengers of the gods, god, angels, guides or ascended masters teaching things that are an imperative to share with other humans. These helpers will lead to the path of the dark ones.
- False teaching systems that does not change or alter the DE1D3 energy system other than within the limits (Kundalini awakening is permitted for the messengers).
- No change in the healing work; only supplying with visions of previous lifetimes and false memories.
- No attempts to "wake up" humans, only delude them into believing they are wakening up, by conditioning programs and promises of a "better future," which should be strived for. The "better future" is based upon human love, money, sex and leisure.
- Resistance against places, persons and energies which could heal and restore the DE1D3 energy system.

The Illuminati and the Foundation of America

As the dark ones took over the core and middle DE1D3 reality field and the DE1D3 were quarantined by the other DE2 races, a faction of the LWBs sided up with the some of the RWBs, which were to some degree active inside the enclosure. At that point the RWBs thought they were doing well, when they in fact were supporting the dark reign due to the fact that the RWBs ran on seriously dimmed down consciousness. Their consciousness abilities were controlled by the inserted dark separation technologies and the LWBs that had had a change of heart, began to undo some of the damages in the RWB energy systems to get a partner in crime against the dark ones inside their own ranks.

As a result, since it was the LWBs that had instigated the freeing processes, they now controlled the RWB energy systems. The LWBs only released what they needed to be able to fight the dark ones and yet be in control of the RWBs inside the enclosure. From what I have experienced regarding the RWBs, the RWBs inside the enclosure are under the control of the deflected LWBs, i.e. the faction under the overall LWBs that deflected from the agenda of the dark ones.

Only the RWBs *outside* the enclosure on the DE2D6 level attached to the outer DE1D3 areas are free of the manipulation schemes of the LWBs. Hence there is no real "good guys" inside the enclosure. The ones that are here are sealed off and thus not in contact with their stellar consciousness or they are dimmed down, being manipulated by the LWBs.

The deflected LWBs discovered the a nightmare they were part of as well as the understanding of their future demise under the control of the dark ones, possessing them one by one to gain their quanta or viable genetics. To get free of the control they teamed up with some of the older reptoid-mammal Sirian B races, the Aryan-Shivas, holding a higher percentage of ancient reptoid genetics than of mammal genetics. The deflected LWBs got, from this collaboration with the Aryan-Shivas, a long needed infusion of 5D reptoid genetics and 6D second generation TEGs, enabling them to work and connect to both the 5th and 6th dimension outside the astral barrier.

Naturally the gift was not shared with the re-activated RWBs they controlled. Most of the possibilities in the RWBs to regain access to the integrated 5D and 6D genetics of their level one energy systems had been removed from the RWBs before activating them.

The deflected LWBs and their kept-under-control RWBs founded a new segment of the brotherhoods called *the planetary hierarchy* or *the enlightened brothers.* The unseen secret level, the top of the planetary hierarchy, consisted of the DE2D6 red robed Minotaurian masters after the story of the Crete Minotauros that controlled the Maze, making it a fitting symbol for the Minotaurian masters considered to be half humanoid (divine) and half animal from the regressed genetics.[69]

In contrast to most of the deflected LWBs, the DE2D6 Minotaurian masters got a higher percentage of the 6D mammal genetics from the DE2D6 reptoid-mammal Aryan-Shivas. The Minotaurian masters and the enlightened brothers became the masterminds behind three key issues unfolded among past and present humans: power, wealth and insight in the covert political and economical levels of the middle DE1D3 areas, giving strategically placed individuals, within the OWO

---

[69] The white bull is also coupled with the Mesopotamian goddess Innanna holding the powers of warfare, sexuality and fertility. The brotherhoods under the dark ones prefer the symbol of Thoth or the bird Anubis, linking them to the god of wisdom in Egypt.

controlled areas, the power to manipulate and change established governmental and societal systems.

The enlightened brothers utilized a strategic manipulation of their volunteering players inside the Maze (the enclosure infused with astral energies) to unfold their agenda, in contrast to the OWO who had mostly focused on controlling humanity through religion, secret knowledge[70], belief systems and governmental politics with the aim of controlling the society. The dark ones only utilize their methods of control, in cases where an important individual either is seen as a threat to them or has viable genetics they want.

The enlightened brothers are the masterminds behind the 5D teachings[71], i.e. controlling the mind through the reptoid genetics in the throat chakra and not via the emotional control of the genetics in the heart chakra under the control of the astral barrier.

The enlightened brothers have created the freemasons and other secret societies in Europe, i.e. the new world and the new order[72]

---

[70] The secret knowledge is naturally false information linking the seeker to the astral plane, where s/he gets totally lost and never discover the true powers.

[71] The mental plane in our day unfold the 5D teachings circulating on the internet using the higher frequency layers of the astral barrier, here called the mental barrier. The game is the same; still diverting humans from the truth. Most conspiracies of today are positioned in the mental plane, as well as most channeling from councils, stellar helpers and similar information leading humanity into the 5th dimension of bliss and happiness as well as the "New Earth" and ascension teachings.

[72] The New World and the New Order, aka the New World Order arises as an idea with the channeled information from the Tibetan to Alice A. Bailey, generating the literate corpus behind most new age teachings today. In most of the books she calls it the new world and the new order, referring to the enlightened brothers inside the political and economical institutions but also referring to the new humanity which will rise in the future. The expression of the new world order is found in the chapter *the Races, the Rays and the and the Signs* in Esoteric Astrology: "This transference out of the lower states of consciousness, expressed through the lower centres, into a higher state, can and will take place in this world period and in this century if humanity so wills it, if the Forces of Light eventually triumph and if **the new world order** comes into being."
http://www.lucistrust.org:8081/obooks/?q=node/482

with the goal of taking back the core and middle DE1D3 areas from the dark ones as well as taking away the power from the avian-reptoid controllers and their draco-reptilian overlords. Their goal was and is to link up to the races under the Sirian B Aryan-Shiva races.[73]

But the unanimity of the enlightened brothers was soon to change given that a sub-faction of the enlightened brothers arose in Europe during the 1600-1700´s. This sub-faction was called the Illuminati.

The Illuminati unfolded during the age of reason, attempting to bring in new ways of thinking into the magi-priestly cooperation of the enlightened brothers. The endeavor to bring in new ways of thinking, giving more freedom to the individual brother as well as his fellow human, divided the enlightened brothers once more. The division led to the freemasonry segment that went to America and created the "new land founded on freedom, liberty and human rights".

The Illuminati brothers instigated *the New Order of the Ages* in America, albeit they kept several allies inside the DE2D4 avian priestly RWB and LWB factions under the Minotaurian masters as well as within the DE2D5 avian-reptoid factions under the draco-reptilian overlords.

I have not talked about the militant draco-reptilian warlords, but they were part of the Reptilian Riots under the draco-reptilian overlords and then afterwards they were mostly kept as a safety net, although they were rarely made use of. The draco-reptilian warlords were working with the DE2D5 avian-reptoid lizards, of which the Illuminati had their alliance. Anyway to get to the next level of the history, we have to alter our perception of things regarding the

---

[73] The Aryan-Shivas are very tall light blue skinned humanlike humanoids, resembling to a striking likeness the Hindu gods as they are depicted today. Some of the enlightened brothers went to India and from here the art of the Hindu gods changed into the likeness of the Aryan-Shivas. The imagery is astrally infused illusions.

America as well. The idea of America as the frontier of the new age stems from the theosophical teachings founded by H.P Blavatsky. H.P. Blavatsky as well as the later A.A. Bailey, i.e. the two ringleaders of the new age teachings of our time, went from their home countries to join *the New Order of the Ages* (the NOA) in America around the late 1800's early 1900's. The aristocratic Russian Mdm. Blavatsky was the first to go, after having toured the East, and later the nobility-rooted Bailey went from England, when a new segment of the teachings needed to be unfolded.[74] Both countries were at that point under the OWO and the two ladies of noble or aristocratic bloodlines - indicating avian-reptoid genetics - were recruited by the NOA to come and join the Illuminati brothers in the freemason societies having created central places of power in the new land of America.

The New Order of the Ages (the NOA)
But before the two ladies went to America a whole other horror show had to unfold to enable the enlightened brothers from Europe to enter the new land.

The original people of North America had, because of their remote location, been left out of the OWO and the races collaborating with the LWBs. Instead they had been in contact with the stellar races descending from the Sirian A lineages through remnants of active genetics. They were unfolding the old teachings, although modified to fit the new generations of original people since most of them had lost their access to the stellar consciousness. Given that the reality field of middle DE1D3 areas had dropped in frequencies, the hara quadrant of the original Americans had slowed down too and had begun pulling in energies from the astral plane, polluting their offshoot Sirian A

---

[74] Blavatsky is said to unfold ray 1 teachings whereas Bailey unfold ray 2 teachings. Blavatsky teachings are mostly based upon secret Buddhist teachings (Kalachakra and the like) whereas Baileys is heavily influenced by esoteric Christian thought systems.

genetics. Hence they were in a state of decay as well. Nevertheless they were still able to connect to the DE3 Sirian A and Maia-Pleiadian races and visitors entered their habitats, doing work there.[75]

To the right is depicted the symbol of the New Order of the Ages from 1782.[76] To be able to come into the new land, the Illuminati brothers had to alter the grid-works of North America. It had to drop significantly to fit the 4D avian signature, which they still held in spite of the 5D genetics and infused 6D TEGs. In order to do so, they instigated a team work with the draco-reptilian warlords for several reasons: the warlords were able to enter North America; not by the use of brute force, but by the use of shimmering or dazzling. The warlords could go into any reality fields, because of an ability they

The icon of the New Order of the Ages (*Annuit Coeptis Novus Ordo Seclorum*) with the all Seeing Eye hovering above the pyramid.

The pyramid symbolizes the OWO or perhaps the planetary hierarchy.

had developed from altering the TEGs they held and by this emitting a type of energy that blocked the consciousness processing of the integrated genetics in other humanoids.[77] On top of this the draco-reptilian warlords once had settlements in the area in ancient times, which gave them access to the gridwork; their genetics resonated with the reality fields of North America. Consequently the warlords entered the soil of America in collaboration with the Illuminati LWBs, still present in Europe. After the warlords had entered, they initiated

---

[75] The story of White Buffalo Calf Women is such a visit.
[76] http://en.wikipedia.org/wiki/Eye_of_Providence
[77] The blocking is perceived as two things: 1) as a strong emission of "wow this person is really handsome, kind and trustworthy type of charisma" and 2) the prevention of all senses of danger. The draco warlords literally dazzle their pray by this emission.

various types of energy work that would alter the gridwork light coding, as they had done it in other reality fields, where they entered with the goal of taking over.[78] In reality fields where the draco-reptilian warlords had entered, the stellar inhabitants, who were able to resist the shimmering, were either slaughtered or traded off to the scavengers. The warlords were the forefront for the draco-reptilian overlords, scouting the areas to see whether or not they were worth taking over. Normally the warlords would link the hijacked reality field to the DE2D5 draco-reptilian gridworks through portals[79] and from here the draco-reptilian overlords could enter.

However in this case the warlords were not interested in opening up to the overlords given that they had deflected to the Illuminati LWBs and joined the collaboration with the goal of gaining control over the new land, where they would be in charge and not serving the draco-reptilian overlords. The warlords were tired of doing all the work and not getting any real power with it, so they joined the new allies instead of their own race. Thus, in agreement with the Illuminati LWBs, they invited a draco-reptilian segment called the Draconians. The Draconians are masters in working with genetics and how to extract them.[80] It is actually a science developed by a faction of the

---

[78] The draco-reptilian warlords do not use military or force by weapons; they use the shimmering method and the pacifying techniques. To some extent they can use "sticks" but they are only used when a stellar being is strong enough to resist their pacifying techniques. I remember these light firing sticks that evaporate your organic form and no, they are not identical with the ones from the movie Stargate. The firing sticks are linked up to the mind of the reptilian and fire by will or intent. They are using reversed light coding to do this, which is part of the TEGs.
[79] Portals differ from dimensional bridges because they are man-made so to speak. They are created by the use of genetics and light coding, accessing the gridwork and from here creating a portal, linking two gridworks together.
[80] I hold a memory of being caught and rounded up to undergo this genetic extraction by two red-green lizard scientists wearing a white lab coat. The memory stems from one of the foreign fragments in my resonance system, which I have removed and sent home.

114

lizard races that have specialized in this but are under the control of the Draconians. The Draconians and draco-reptilian warlords rounded up the original people of America[81] with the intent of extracting the Sirian A offshoot genetics, still being part of their energy systems. The new alliance needed to lift out of the regressed state to enable them to become smarter than the draco-reptilian overlords. Thus the deal with the Illuminati LWBs was rewarding for both the Draconians and the warlords, giving them back their freedom, a new improved set of genetics and the power over new landmasses. Instead of being the warriors raiding and taking over land for the overlords, the warlords became landowners. Now they just had to get the gridwork running with energies allowing the Illuminati LWBs to enter.

The reality fields of North America had been kept close to their original colonial state by the original Americans and this had to change for the Illuminati brothers to enter.

This is where the massive slaughtering of the original Americans began, the wars between the original people and the pioneers, the use of military force and so forth along with the inhuman treatment of afro-American slaves that were a part of the same time-frame from the 16th throughout the 19th centuries.[82]

The brutality secured the accessibility[83] for the Illuminati LWBs and they have kept this position to this day by creating the visible and invisible military forces, experiments in Milabs, weapon industry etc. They are taking part of all wars in the world, or creating them, to keep their energetic status quo in a land that still hold many viable genetics

---

[81] They are still utilizing the natives as well as their descendants holding the original native genetics both inside and outside the "Indian" reservations to this day.

[82] https://en.wikipedia.org/wiki/Population_history_of_indigenous_peoples_of_the_Americas

[83] Why does brutality and murder of living beings give access for regressed races? That has to do with the genetics they developed under the Reptilian Riots, which added a strain of primitive brute energy to their genetics. They need to "seed" this into the gridworks of the field they want to take over to be able to exist there.

and therefore could return to its natural state. As long as the natural people of the land are present, the land can heal itself. It is thus understandable why the Illuminati LWBs and their governmental departments are keeping the original Americans under conditions that are under all forms of critique (not that Denmark did better with the people of Greenland).

Many of the abductions are based upon Americans that hold the original American genetics in some form. The Illuminati brothers need the reptoid-mammal Sirian A genetics to counteract their stellar avian genetics and to be able to connect to the 5D reptoid-mammal reality fields as well as being able to exist in a land that does not belong to them. Genetic manipulations to be able to go into a reality field, which is not indigenous to the genetics, are taking place all over this quadrant, hence the trade of the genetics from the DE1D3 areas.

Regrettably for the Illuminati LWBs, many of them have returned to ritualistic magic in search of individual power, connecting them back to the top of the LWBs, i.e. the Minotaurian masters, which then means that their separation as such is nullified; the Illuminati brothers of the US and Europe are still one unity.

The warlords are working with the Illuminati LWBs as part of the controlled secret government of the US to this day, however new reptoid and Aryan-Shiva races are entering the scene pushing out the old generations of warlords and the old NOA. For this reason a battle has been going between the new segment of the NOA and the old segment of NOA. Because of this some of the warlords and their Draconian allies are returning to the reptoid fold, leaving the NOA coalition behind. The new segment of NOA work with the new stellar-earth humanity programs, making it possible for the middle DE1D3 area organic form to enter the host-fields of the DE2D4 and DE2D5 new stellar races. All in all old NOA is shifting to the new segment of the NOA coalition.

The Technologies in Humans

First and foremost it is important to acknowledge two facts:

- Since the dark ones are leaving, only a few remains, the feeding technologies are mostly inactive and thus they can be removed without any problems. Unless, naturally it is owned by a draco-reptilian or a dark one still present in the DE2D4 areas linked up to the middle DE1D3 enclosure.[84]

- All inserted technologies are individual and depend on the type of genetics present in the chakras, put there to manufacture specific outcomes to supply the races, which have taken part of the programs running inside the enclosure.

The Dreamtime Technologies

Every night the DE1D3 energy system and the observing principle of the organic form (the ego) shift out of the organic form and enter many other types of sub-fields generated for the purpose. Here the DE1D3 energy system and the ego continue the processing of energy, generating a plethora of conditioned genetics that can be gathered and harvested for various purposes.

In dream-time the DE1D3 energy system and the ego shift from the organic form and into its dream-body. The dream-body is a sub-form consisting of astral energies and is positioned in the astral plane.

The dream-body is only produced as long as the chakras and the aura participate in the astral plane and by this are infused with astral energies upheld by the astral grid in the quantum morphogenetic

---

[84] This is a whole other level of information and I will not go further into this, the reason why they are stay there etc.

field. Hence conscious astral travel in meditation is the shifting from the daytime awareness of the organic form into the dream-body. Here the astral traveler enters the astral plane full of illusions and thoughtforms generated for the purpose of making people believe in the spirituality programs.[85]

The first level to cleanse out, to be able to get to the fragments put into the highest level of the chakras,[86] is the energies producing dreams, visions and sensations that are weird and full of typical dreamlike stuff.

Different programs are linked up to the chakras and they unfold in dreamtime, when we are out of the organic form and have entered the dream-body. Here the ego, as the recorder and observer, takes part of realities which the astral energies in the chakras pull the observer into. In these sub-realities the ego experiences the complete emotional range from fear to sadness, happiness, anger and so forth. Psychologists have interpreted this as subconscious material in need of processing. This is true to a certain extent, which becomes clear after having worked with the chakras for a long time.

As the chakras are cleansed out of the first level of astral energies, i.e. normal subconscious material, they enter into their function as

---

[85] Spirituality programs are astrally based and humans exercising these energies, thinking they are very spiritual, often end up having problems in the areas around the solar plexus. The programs are engineered to make the ego get lost in the illusions and astral energies and the more the ego, generated by the solar plexus chakra, links up to the astral plane, the more clogged the chakra gets, which in the end leads to illnesses as cancer and similar problems of the pancreas, liver, spleen, intestines, kidneys etc, i.e. all of the organs being part of the metabolic system of the body.

[86] Each chakra holds many sublevels of frequencies, all reflecting the many astral sub-fields they are able to link up to, depending on beliefsystems etc. The chakras were originally able to work on several vibration and radiation levels because a reality field holds many sub-fields where consciousness can be evolved and transform energy. This ability has been transferred to the astral plane instead. Thus cleansing of chakras take years to accomplish since all belief systems have to be altered or removed to free the chakras of the astral energies linking them up to the astral plane.

energy generators and resonance tools making the dream-body adjust to the sub-fields of the astral plane. When the chakras reach this level of their function the dreams change and become just as real as the daily life.

Here the ego is participating in settings that fully resemble the daily life and what is experienced there; however these sub-fields are part of the astral plane, albeit in a higher frequency, unfolding real life scenarios as well as linking to the reintegration field, e.g. the schools taking place there. The interaction with the real life sub-fields of the astral plane makes the chakras believe that they are part of a true reality and thus unfold their content of energies with the purpose of transforming the fragmented genetics in the chakras. Most of the real life sub-fields are part of the programs conditioning the genetic fragments into being able to become part of TEGs for the human clones.

The original DE1D3 energy system only consists of vibration and radiation energies. They are set to unfold a specific range of energy to resonate with the surrounding field of the DE1D3 system. However to avoid the DE1D3 energy system to perform its ability to elevate and generate energy, making it possible for the genetics of the energy system to connect to the organic form and by this integrate the knowledge of the upper triangle, fragmented genetics from other energy systems are inserted into the chakras.

The fragments interact with the energies of the chakras as if they were still part of the original energy system, albeit they are from another energy system, which then distorts the chakras since they are processing light coding from two energy systems. This prevents the genetics of the sealed off energy system from connecting with the DE1D3 energy system (the hara quadrant) and not before we are rid of the inserted fragments can we begin the incorporation of our own knowledge and genetics.

In dreamtime the fragmented genetics continue to link up to *the other chakra systems*, the inserted genetics are interconnected with, and the ego can accidently shift from the normal dream-body into the dream-body of the additional chakra systems, producing perception of and interaction with the sub-fields the genetics inserted here are interacting with.

Thus the participation in real life sub-fields can also be a result of the fragmented genetics, enabling us to become part of the other chakra systems we are interlinked to, through the original personality field of the original energy system the bits stem from.

An example

For at long time I have taken part in "normal settings of a human", where my ego experience things that I might as well could have experienced in this organic form, except from the fact that my ego is clear and observing, wondering and questioning during the whole dream-state. There is no ego-identification with the settings, and my ego is painfully aware of being part of a scenario that it should not take part in. The moment before I wake up, my ego always know that "now I will be pulled out and never return to this body and reality again". I am taking part in different bodies and scenarios each night. Thus my observing principle of the solar plexus, the ego, is shifting between the organic form I keep returning to, as the holder of the DE1D3 energy system, and the plethora of dream-bodies that are different every night, linked up to the inserted genetics of my chakra system. I am yet to discover the removal technology of the inserted fragments on this level.[87]

---

[87] Trust me I have tried to cleanse these fragments out over and over again, but there are levels I cannot access yet, so daily energy work on this, to get to the level where they are stored is needed to solve this problem. But understanding of dynamics is always the beginning of solving the 1000 or more programs we are taking part of,

The Entity Generating and Feeding Programs

But it does not end there. If the correct type of fragmented genetics is inserted into the chakras, they can connect to *the entity generating programs*.

As the fragments are activated, they emit vibration and radiation energies. The vibration and radiation energies are then stored in sack extending from the genetic bit in the chakra through energy cords, which can only be seen when the correct vibration and radiation level of the chakras are activated. If one of the sacks is dissolved, by pulling out the genetic bit from the chakra, then the sack bursts, the genetic bit and the vibration and radiation energies merge together and then rise up as a sort of entity.

From this I have concluded that each sack generates the pre-stage of a holographic entity[88] that are engineered to take on a form on the astral plane or in other systems, utilizing the human psyche as the conditioning principle. The experiences during dreamtime imprint the genetic bit with the present level of consciousness through the ways the dream-ego act, behave and do during dreamtime. These entities are then harvested and put into human chakra systems, clones perhaps,[89] where they are controlling the ego and chakra systems on a subconscious level. Others are transferred to new reality fields,

---

built into the DE1 reality fields by the many races having had their experiments here, of which the latest is the astral barrier and feeding programs of the dark ones.

[88] Devas, fairies, nature spirits and similar energy entities can be a product of this technology if they for some reason are not harvested and inserted into an energy system.

[89] I got the information, I do not know if it is correct, that half of the population on Earth is clones of level one energy systems, not having a level one energy system of their own. The clones are entirely the product of the harvested energies and cloned genetics from other level one energy systems. Adding this to the fact of the many burned out level one energy systems, and the dumped one, in the reintegration areas and cycles, it is of no real surprise why most of humanity is not interested in change, but prefer things as status quo. Clones and burned out energy systems have no incentive to progress and change.

where they become the personality of a bio-android form, such as the Grays. Consequently there is a trade going on.

But the technology is also part of the feeding programs of the dark ones, being the food supply for the dark ones. The dark ones literally ingest these pre-stage entities gathered in the sacks. When the sacks are ready to be harvested, the "skin" of the sack is removed and the pre-stage entity rises up. Then it is led to a dark one that through the means of horizontal merging[90] incorporates the pre-stage entity into his or her energy system. This will keep the dissolving energy system going for a while, a day or two, and then a new pre-stage entity is needed to feed the energy system of a dark one. Without the infusion of the pre-stage entity, the energy system of a dark one will dissolve, because s/he has burned up their template, holding the fuelling genetics, a long time ago.

The Dark Technologies
There are dark separation technologies added to the level one energy system. The seals are put in to prevent the integrated genetics in the energy system from connecting to the template genetics, wake up and be able to leave our reality field. Besides of the seals there are the fragmented genetics put into the chakras to make them run on incorrect light coding sequences, altering the light coding of the heart chakra and thus preventing it from linking to the heart vortex and from here accessing the vibration field. The same is the case with the throat chakra linked to the throat vortex and from here accessing the radiation field as well as the root chakra, denying it access to the root vortex and the quantum morphogenetic field.

---

[90] Horizontal merging is where one energy system adjusts to another energy system and then light coding and genetic information can be exchanged between the two systems.

I have talked about the front and back side of the DE1D3 energy system in my videos on YouTube and the dark technology attached to the chakras to steer them in certain directions. This technology I have still not fully figured out what the purpose was.

However since I could remove all of this technology without any problems, it could indicate that they were remnants of foreign stellar races having had a specific program running inside the enclosure and now have left, leaving behind their machinery. Or perhaps this technology was part of the adaptation technology that dimmed down the chakras and removed the upper chakras. If this technology is part of the chakra system, it has to be removed as well.

There are many variations of dark technology inserted into the aura, the chakras, the level one energy system and so forth; all from astral bugs to advanced dark technology that has to be removed by methods resembling surgery, using vibration and radiation energies (light coding) as the tools. In these cases, developed consciousness abilities are required to carry out the holographic operation as well as knowing when to use vibration or radiation energies and how.

Dark technology *can only be removed if* the dark one, having inserted the technology, has abandoned the energy system or gives his or her permission. The latter is done by trade of something they want, or by the healer being part of some type of council or group holding a high rank within the communities of the collaborating dark ones and LWBs. *I am here saying that only the ones collaborating with the dark ones can remove operative dark technology.*

If we attempt to remove it and succeed, we are attacked for as long as it pleases the dark one, or they take what they feel is theirs from our energy system, draining us dry. Thus if we, as healers, are confronted with dark technology the first thing we look for is if it is in operation or has been abandoned. Not before this is cleared out, do we begin working with the dark technologies. It is easy to know if it is

123

operative because if it is in use, the dark one will show up in our mind the moment we look into the energy system of our client. It can seem hard that we are forced to decline assisting humans in need of our help, but even though we have reached the level, where the dark ones leave us alone and we leave them alone due to the old rules of engagement between the LPRF3s[91] and similar groups, the decision not to help always has to be seen in the bigger picture, understanding the consequences of helping versus not helping.[92]

The Incubation Technologies

The incubation technologies are part of the new stellar races and other present day participants of the programs run in the middle DE1D3 areas, utilizing the DE1D3 energy system for many purposes.

New types of technologies have been invented to generate viable genetics to uphold the wearing out gene pool of these races.

This arose as the non-crystalline and other races discovered that their breed out and selected racial traits led to a wearing out of their gene pool. To grow new genetics, a definite portion of humanity was selected, by deals with the LWBs etc, to become incubators of viable genetics since they held the ancient stellar energy system that could unfold these genetics.

As we shall see the DE2D4/DE2D6 non-crystalline and the DE2D5 new stellar races do not want the full energy system to awaken, due to the pre-disposition to unfold the infection, so their work is not

---

[91] I have not gone into the rules of engagement amongst the original LPRF3s or the agreements made between the RWBs from outside the enclosure and the LWBS, since these only apply for humanoids of these groups. The rules of engagement and other laws can be very difficult for outsiders to understand, not having been around in the game as long as the ones taking part of these groups.

[92] If we as healers assist one holding operative dark technology and we are taken out for good, then all the others we could have helped will not get our assistance and in the long run, one person can never outweigh the cause of helping as many as possible.

aimed at awakening their ancestral siblings. However they are able to use the non-awakened humans as their incubators and suppliers of genetics.

Instead of only inserting fragments from another energy system to distort the chakras, two additional chakras were added to the DE1D3 energy system holding the seed of the genetics that needed (and needs since these technologies are still in operation) to be matured and grown. These chakras are mostly placed above the heart chakra as a second chakra or just below the throat chakra. Sometimes an artificial ajna chakra is added as well. These chakras are placed on frequencies that the ego is unable to access.

When the time is ripe the full-fledged genetics are removed either during sleep or by abduction and new genetics to be developed are inserted. Many types of genetics have been groomed this way and the latest experiment I have seen were genetics being grown to be able to access the dimensional bridges of the Sirian A reality fields, which run on genetic recognition. These experiments are part of the US military complex (the test subject lived in Germany) and are aimed at getting the ability to enter the dimensional bridges in the present human form.

Understanding the Effects of the Astral Barrier
The last thing we need to address to see the complete story is to understand the effects of the astral barrier and what happens if is not removed.

Astral energies, producing the astral barrier, are light coding having been reversed further from the LPU settings along with other types of energy. The reversed light coding fueling the astral barrier or the astral plane, since these two things are the same, grew out of the enclosure.

The enclosure was the result of a blueprint created to encircle the core and middle DE1D3 areas and operating distortion technologies messing with the core crystals. The distortion technologies, unfolding the blueprint into the gridworks, reversed the light coding of the core and middle DE1D3 areas, and by this making the core and middle sections repulse the outer DE1D3 areas, or sort of separate them by the way the light coding worked. Instead of producing the normal holographic dynamics of the LPU we are part of, the energies of the enclosure were standing in a steady state mode, strongly enforced by the quarantine.

However the quarantine has been lifted and the infusion of light coding from adjacent reality fields are part of the resetting of the DE1D3 areas. An uncomplicated resetting can only take place if humanity follows the pull to change their chakra systems and how they utilize the energies connected hereto. If humanity does not do the changes, the heave between the resetting energies and the opposing energies in humanity will generate counteracting forces. These forces will lead to a point where the differences in the energy fields of the collective sum of humans will act as deadweight for the resetting core and middle DE1D3 areas and by this the main energy fields of the areas will lift leaving the deadweight behind.

The process of separating humanity has already begun. It has been called the bifurcation of timelines[93] which means that one set of humanity will accelerate their consciousness, whereas another level of humanity will become the deadweight. The humans choosing not to adapt to the changes will experience different timelines than the ones accepting the changes and follow the pull. How this will play out in the future on the physical level is uncertain but the main effects are:

---

[93] By Lisa Renee. The same dynamics have been mentioned by Bashar, Simon Parkes and alike.

- The pulling out of viable genetics by the new stellar races from the humans that do not follow the resetting process has already begun. This is done to secure their property (the genetics).
- This will lead to physical decay of the organic body in these humans since they do not have any upholding genetics in the level one energy system. When the level one energy system does not work, the chakra system stops to work properly and the body breaks down like an old car, where the bits and pieces stop working.
- When these humans die, their body, the chakra system and the level one energy system will dissolve into dust.
- This dust will attach to the deadweight timelines pulling them further down in vibration. When this happens the deadweight timelines will accelerate their decay and the humans linked to them will die more rapidly and so forth until all deadweight timelines and their connected humans have turned into dust.
- After this only the ones with viable genetics in their level one energy system will continue existing in the DE1D3 areas.

The astral energies began as an effect of the steady state energies in the gridworks added with diversion energies from the fragmented genetics inserted into the chakras. The astral energies are infused with the infected energies as well utilized by the humanoids adapting to the consciousness of the dark ones. From 1548 the connection between the humans inside the enclosure[94] and the humanoids in the

---

[94] Before 2500 BCE I call the middle DE1D3 inhabitants for earth humanoids. After 2500 BCE with the rise of the enclosure and the dark reign I call them humans due to the high level of astral energies. The astral energies of the chakra system generate a sort of grid in us and this separates us from other humanoids of the LPU. The astral grid is attached to the quantum morphogenetic field. It is thus no longer the astral

outer DE1D3 areas were cut off and humans have from that period sustained and upheld the astral barrier themselves by their ways of thinking and feeling.

The astral barrier or astral plane consist of thoughtforms and sub-programs engineered to unfold a specific range of frequencies, which is what we today perceive as emotional and mental impulses, but also ideas ranging from scientific to new age ideas. The dark ones have throughout their reign changed the sub-programs according to the changes instigated by the OWO and the lizards when needed.

The astral barrier produce inner visions, religious visions, sightings of Virgin Mary, Jesus, angels, demons, archangels, the present day concept of the ascended masters and so forth. Perception of a higher entity with many names all from God to Allah etc. is also part of the maintenance programs of the astral barrier. All thoughts of magic, powers, entities to be called upon, invocations, incantations, tarot cards, potions, herbal remedies, small bags with herbs, bones and spell-bound objects are also part of the maintenance programs of the astral barrier and they all clog the solar plexus, draining the DE1D3 energy system of its energy; hence the many illnesses and problems with the heart, liver, spleen, pancreas, intestines, stomach etc, often seen in people having exercised spirituality for a long time.

To ensure that all humans maintained the astral barrier through their chakra systems, i.e. through all of the above use of astral energies, the energy emissions from the DE1D3 energy system have been enhanced by the activation of strong emotions, positive and negative, to sexual energies fueled by lust and perversions.

The emotional urge to take in mind-altering substances such as alcohol, drugs, mushrooms and similar substances are all leaving the

---

barrier and the enclosure that is preventing us from reaching outside the middle areas, but the internal grid of astral energies. We can penetrate the astral barrier, if we want since the dark ones are gone and thus no longer keep the programs running.

solar plexus open to possessions and integration of astral entities,[95] connecting the chakra system even stronger to the astral plane.

Mind-altering medication is given to make humans attach stronger to the astral plane, for various purposes and reasons. One is if the level one energy system has reached its limits of non-viable genetics and has to shift from the areas where the level one energy systems go to and into the astral plane. Illness and medication is often utilized in such cases, where a previous functional level one energy system wears out during integration into an organic form.

A high intake of refined sugar lowers the pH value and destroys the energetic balance of the cells, preventing them from accessing the energies outside the astral plane. Processed food with high levels of chemicals generates a dimmed down DE1D3 energy system making it more prone to react to the astral energies of the barrier.

Movies, entertainment and all that we perceive to be things that humans do, are part of the maintenance programs of the astral barrier. As long as humans cling to their "humanity" they are kept inside the enclosure; this is luckily changing due to the dark ones leaving.

Thus in daytime spiritual and religious people are maintaining the astral barrier by their constant interaction with the astral energies utilizing *the middle programs* of the barrier. It should be duly noted that scientific oriented people utilize *the upper programs* bordering to the "mental areas" of the barrier, whereas illiterate and non-educated people use *the lowest levels of the programs* in the

---

[95] Astral entities are all of the various lifeforms the astral plane houses. These are created by genetic fragments that for some reason end without any energy system. The astral energies then gather around the genetic bit and eventually an entity arises. Some of the entities are created by magicians and similar energy workers to enable them to affect other humans, their surroundings etc in a specific way. Here the magician takes of his or her integrated genetics and create an astral entity.

barrier.[96] The new stellar races and the non-crystalline soul races do not need the astral barrier; only the crystalline races do because their crystalline technology is the inverted version of the maintenance programs of the astral barrier. The crystalline agenda literally needs the astral barrier to transform the enclosure into their version of reality.

---

[96] When we evolve the brain, we follow the programs of the barrier from the lowest to the highest types of programs all running on specific reversed light coding ensuring that the DE1D3 energy system produce the energies to fuel the thoughtforms needed to uphold the chosen beliefsystems.

The Missions into the Less-Progressive Universe

The missions had many purposes. It is too simple just to say that the soul races entered with the goal of "saving" anybody or to assist the deflected soul races; nothing could be further from the truth. When I wrote the prospect of the fourth course, I was under the ideas of older material and as I have traversed through the history as it has unfolded to me, my understanding has expanded as well as become more nuanced.

First and foremost the initial travelers into the LPU from the HRF3 areas of the holographic metaverse (the HMDE3) entered to take part of the scientific projects in the Sirian workstations. Some reptoid soul races went into the Maldakian settlements to explore the possibilities of the new light coding sciences, which were performed there.

After the timeline event the missions changed into what could be called rescue missions, although there were only few attempts and then the project of rescuing was abandoned given the fact that it was impossible to rescue anybody.

The change of the less-progressive substances into an entirely new version of light coding in the DE2 system as well as the merged-in TEGs and the arisen dark areas made the rescue missions patronizing, since the DE2 ancient stellar races had adjusted to the post-timeline circumstances. All that was left for the HMDE3s was to instigate the programs of the new colonies and then await the inhabitants of the changed level of the DE2 system to come around and begin the transformation process themselves, by their own free will and by the means that had been given to them. This was agreed upon from the higher leveled races of the LPU and the HM.

Thus the DE2s were left on their own to evolve and work with the holographic settings that had been generated by the timeline event and the rest of the HMDE3s left except from the ones connected to the colonies having seeded the holographic teachings. They also gave programs of progression to the races of the Sirius A lineages and their new DE3 system. The DE3s had been put in charge of the DE2 systems in forms of councils and overseeing projects by the higher leveled LPU races and the leaving HMDE3s, although not many of the programs have been heard of in our vicinity due to the Reptilian Riots and the reign of the dark ones.

Done is done and the goal for us is to understand and then take up the lead and the work that were left for us to do: transforming the DE2 holographic energy system and return to the original less-progressive settings, i.e. activate the template and the energy system, integrate the genetics and from here reconstruct the first LPU energy system. After this reconstruction the next level awaits us, i.e. to re-model the LPU energy system into a HMDE3 energy system and by this regain control over our HMDE3 genetics. That is for the second year of the education and we need to do this to be able to travel through the dimensional bridges of the DE2 system back into the timelines of the Sirius A system, which are still there as well as regaining access to the holographic teachings to be able to enter the bridge zones back to the HM.[97]

Entering the Sirian Workstations

The HRF3s entered the LPU before the timeline event as orbs holding the merged light coding and light units from the HM. The entering into the LPU was based upon *a choice or free will* and not by the laws of the cycles. The entering could be done by direct integration, where

---

[97] More about this later on.

the form of the HRF3 was dissolved and only the orb entered the Sirian workstations where a new form and a level one energy system were generated to be able to exist inside the LPRF3 Sirius system. The soul genetics were also modified in the LPRF3 Sirian workstations and then integrated in into the level one energy system and template for the purpose of allowing the progression possibilities of the mixed core in the Sirius system to unfold naturally into the new energy system.

The HRF3 form and personality could also choose to generate a copy of the orb, where the soul genetics in the original orb were cloned and then put into a new orb holding the first versions of the TEGs from the HM. The orb with the cloned genetics would then enter the LPU and the soul genetics and the TEGs would again be modified to fit the settings of the Sirius system as well as unfolding the capacities needed to do the job. The entering orb, i.e. soul as we understand it, with its soul genetics held the knowledge and abilities it had developed in the HM as well as a sense of self. The entering orb connected to the less-progressive light coding in the reality field it wanted to explore or work in.

In both cases the template and energy system were generated and the orb, holding the soul genetics from the HM, would shed off the HM light coding and integrate the soul genetics into the template of the LPU; that is the ones that were not to be utilized right away. The other genetics with TEGs became the integrated genetics determining the personality and function of the level one energy system.

Therefore the orb, either the integrated or the clone, unfolded a certain amount of the soul genetics into the three main vortexes to be able to activate the energy system. More correctly the possibilities and probabilities of the soul genetics generated the vortexes from which the energy system could unfold as existence inside the LPU.

Then more LPU light coding were pulled in and the quantum morphogenetic field was created, i.e. the blueprint for the form. The soul genetics in the template and the integrated genetics in the three main vortexes were engineered to enable the energy system to work as needed and to be able to pull in the correct amount of radiation and vibration energies making the radiation and vibration auric fields work.

The integration into the LPU was possible through the agreements made with the councils of the HRF3s as well as the LPRF3 and LPRF4s and thus any integration into the LPU was determined, unfolded and executed through the assistance of the groups of LPU and HM races, which had been placed in the bridging zones.

The goal was always to return to the HM after a period (and many did) and develop the gained sciences and knowledge further in the HRF3 communities to solve some of the problems holding the root in the Internal Strife.

The Present and the Future

In the last chapters we look into the LPU races, their involvement of our present lives and into the future. We look into the races and their versions of genetics. Much has already been written during the first section, and thus the last chapters round up this information.

The genetics are what connect all types of organic lifeforms in the densities and reality fields together. The genetics are the means to all existence, knowledge etc in all of the dimensions and gridworks. They are the foundation of a personality and the sense of self and much more.

The last part of this book is finished with the general level, where we summarize all of the details of the settings and what else shows up.

Ending the Dark Reign

The Beginning of the End

During the 1980'ties and up until the year 2013 the non-crystalline races of the DE2D4 and DE2D6 took part in the pursuit to get rid of the dark reign but also to warn us against the next level of what was coming our way.[98]

The insectoid stellar races (the Grays) in the outskirts of the DE1D3 had their own agenda to groom, unfolding their hybrid programs and being busy harvesting as much insectoid genetics as possible.[99] At the same time various races under the crystalline DE2D6 Sirian Bs (not the Shivas) were seeding thoughtforms of the 12-stranded template, the DE2 silicate body and the technologies of DNA activation.[100] In spite of the differences in the goals of the agendas, they all took part in ending the dark reign and freeing the DE1D3 reality field of their

---

[98] Here I specifically think about Alex Collier and others like him preparing us for the future but without the 12-stranded ideology.

[99] In one of the chakra readings I have done, it was informed that our DE1DE3 area had developed their version of the android form, we call Grays or Dows. Given that the Gray android form is present in most stellar communities, this is not a surprise when we think of it. The Grays are caretakers or janitors for the other stellar races, coming into a reality field, settle and then leave the projects to unfold on their own. The Grays are left behind to oversee the projects and that they unfold according to plan. Some of the Grays that were left behind on our reality field are present outside the enclosure, in the areas holding the science labs and facilities under the reptoid races collaborating with the LWBs and the draco-reptilian overlords. To this day, these Grays consider themselves to be the keepers and they take this very seriously. They know that they are DE1D3 created and as such they see themselves as the true inhabitants of this reality field.

[100] All working under the umbrella of the Sirian B Guardian Alliances and similar ideologies of the silicate matrix, Kryst, Cosmic Christ, crystalline, DNA activation, 12-stranded template etc.

suppressors. The same groups have freed other non-free stellar races in the DE3-DE2 sectors that fell under the reign of the dark ones. All in all the dark antagonistic core is getting smaller for each reality field that returns to its original holographic setting, that is the less-progressive setting from after the timeline event and before the regression and the Reptilian Riots.

On top of this, the draco-reptilian overlords, as a race, have played their part in the LPU history and are now in remission and have been for a while. They have reached their potential age and are shifting out of their present reptilian form and into a whole new type of organic form in the made-up dimensions of the LPU made possible by genetic engineering done in e.g. the programs of the middle DE1D3 areas. The draco-reptilian overlords are soon history.

The distortion and reversal technologies used by the dark ones and the Dracos, altering the DE3-DE2 reality fields of the LPU, are vanishing from the DE3-DE2 sectors and the various stellar races of the imprisoned reality fields under the scavengers, the many reality fields under the dominion of the draco-reptilian overlords as well as the areas under the dark ones are undergoing the next evolutionary steps of the LPU history. But what does this freeing process really mean? What are the DE3-DE2 new stellar races[101] up to and what does this mean to us? The few ancient stellar races that originated within the various DE3-DE2 reality fields after the timeline event, and did not regress or were killed during the Reptilian Riots, have been captured by the scavengers, fragmented or brought here as food for the dark ones or possible genetic suppliers for the LWBs.

---

[101] When I call them the DE3-DE2 new stellar races instead of just the DE2 new stellar races, it is because of the supreme councils positioned in the outskirts of the DE2 entering the post-timeline event areas of the DE3. New technologies permit them to dimensionally enter these reality fields in spite of the fact that they are only holding to the highest DE2D6 genetics.

Most of them have been sealed off and left to be forgotten inside the reincarnation cycles as the LWBs stopped having use of them. For them the freeing process means that they are able to return to their home systems, if they are capable to reactive the remaining integrated genetics and restore them; that is the ones which still have a functional upper and lower template or templates that can become functional.[102] However the returning to their home systems is not without problems because the ancient stellar races are of a different set up than the present races of the DE2 and DE3 systems.

Most of the LPU new stellar races have undergone an evolutionary process built upon many new generations of the TEGs and similar technologies changing the light coding of their energy systems into something new. The post-timeline energy system and its template in the captured humanoids do not resemble the structure of the new stellar races of today.

Thus difficult decisions are to be made with the old templates and their genetics and who is to make that decision? The personality of the sealed off template with its genetics, then put down into a hibernated state, is out of order to decide anything unless the seals are removed.

From what I have seen the players of the freeing process are not interested in removing the seals of their former imprisoned brothers and sisters present in the middle DE1D3 areas. To the new stellar races of the freeing process this type of consciousness and knowledge is unwarranted. The ancient genetics and the dormant personality is not a "real being" in their eyes compared to the standards of present day communities. However this does not stop them from wanting the

---

[102] The ones under the control of the remaining draco-reptilians or the dark ones cannot free themselves before they are let loose of their controllers. But in the future as these factions leave too, they will cut loose their property and then the level one energy systems can be restored.

genetics in the template; they just do not want the integrated and conditioned genetics linked to the personality of the energy system. Another factor is the predisposed genetics, i.e. the genetics with the merged-in TEGs which had a tendency to break down and gave ground for the dark ones to take over to begin with.

The Survivors of the Infection

The solutions to the predisposed genetics running in the gene pool of the DE2D5 races and non-crystalline DE2D4 races have been based upon the technologies of the second generation TEGs, modified and altered to fit the purpose of the ones that did not get infected. The surviving groups of races; i.e. the descendants of the groups that held less modified soul genetics with TEGs to begin with, have suppressed the predisposed genetics by breading out this type of genetics.

This has naturally left the DE3-DE2 sector with a clinically altered gene pool that, to the dismay of these stellar races, are starting to weaken because only few of the original possibilities and probabilities of the ancient stellar races are unfolding; all in all their breeding programs are going against the blueprint of their reality field. [103]

Progression for all of the DE3-DE2 stellar races can only take place if the khundarays of the reality field unfolds all of the potentials into the possibilities and probabilities of the races living there and the clinically altered gene pool prevents this. As a consequence the selected gene pool is not being infused with the energies from the khundarays and the genetic set up is weakening leaving the new stellar races with a new problem. They are in dire need of infusions

---

[103] Light coding progression fields (the quantum flux fields) generate the blueprint of all reality fields, having encoded the probabilities and possibilities of that reality field into the holographic light coding of the gridworks. The progression fields set the vibration and radiation levels determining the dimensional energies of the field in question and by this selecting what type of genetics that are able to unfold there.

with the older type of genetics and it is here the freeing of the DE1D3 reality fields and the ancient stellar races becomes important for their survival and their future.

The Solutions
Because of these issues many of *the ancient stellar races* will not be awakened. Instead solutions have been made without their consent and are executed during the period of 2012-2025:

1) *Their genetics are being harvested by their descendants*: The imprisoned humanoids in the middle DE1D3 areas have been utilized as energy and genetics suppliers for so long, that the new stellar races see them as defected energy systems; nevertheless the genetics of the template are fine enough to be pulled out, leaving the energy system to decay along with the section of the middle DE1D3 areas under the astral barrier. The genetics are then put into the model of the new stellar races, altering the template genetics into present day versions being able to fuel the new energy systems.

2) *They are undergoing a transformation process*: This model is chosen for the most viable genetics and energy systems. The sealed off template and energy system are not awakened but are altered into a new type of working class under the new stellar races, having specialized in hierarchical communities where the highest ranked humanoids hold the most advanced TEGs and soul genetics and below them exist all sorts of sub-classes being engineered to fit specific scientific tasks. The new stellar races are taking the sealed off template and energy systems and attach them to new organic forms, after having wiped out the memories of the personality, unfolded through different genetic programs. Yes, the family members[104] are

---

[104] I call them this, because many of the messages from the present soul races to us are sayings like: "you are our family", "we are genetically related" and so forth.

freeing their forefathers from the reign of the dark ones, but only to put them under a new type of tyranny.

3) *Or the ancient stellar humanoids are awakened and left for the scavengers in the lesser protected zones, i.e. the drop zones.* The lesser protected zones are part of the DE2 system, where the previous workers of the prison fields around the DE3-DE2 systems have been or are being dumped to "build new reality fields on their own after their own liking".

A very fine sales speech although the truth be told, this means that they are being left to their own means and demise in *the drop zones*. Without the new technology and the light coding to follow the set of light coding (khundaray flows) of the DE3-DE2 sectors, being altered to fit the genetics of the new stellar races, the stellar races from the prison systems stand a slim chance of survival. However this turned out to be a miscalculation from the new stellar races in the future.[105] Most of the stellar races that are dumped on the "new reality fields to unfold their own free worlds" hold a high degree of soul genetics and in the near future they will connect to the holographic metaverse through genetic telepathy with the Sirian A races in the HMDE3 reality fields.

4) *To solve the issue with the predisposed genetics in solution one and two*, the new stellar races alter the predisposed genetics by pulling them out of the template and re-engineer them before they are reinstated into a new energy system within their communities or they are dumped, if this cannot take place.

All in all: Solution one, two and four leave the personality sealed off or wiped clean of the memories – it has not been active for centuries anyway – taking home the viable template genetics to

---

[105] Some of these dumped races are the ones that become the true resistance movement in the future, working against both the new stellar races and the CSBs with the goal of reinstating the ancient stellar humanoid energy system.

infuse the wearing out gene-pool with viable genetics in the new stellar communities. Solution three leaves the template intact, the energy system and the personality is freed and gets the chance to gather a new organic form in the drop zones, as they are called. The races, which advocate for the DE1D3 to become a drop zone, consider humanity to hold all of the genetics they do not want, similar to other freed prison fields, and they prefer the imprisoned races to evolve a new type of species on their own.

The Crystalline Races

Another factor in the freeing process of Earth is the DE2D6 crystalline Sirian Bs and their allies (the CSBs). This faction is in opposition to the other avian-reptoid-mammal new stellar races in our quadrant. The DE2D4 non-crystalline races work against the CSBs and the reptoid-mammal stellar races of the DE2D5 (having freed themselves from the dominion of the draco-reptilian overlords) are fighting the CSBs in open wars in the interdimensional cross-zones between the DE2D5 and DE2D6 reality fields. Why are the other stellar races in such an opposition to the crystalline DE2D6 Sirian Bs?

The answer lies within the crystalline technology and the silicate template. Whereas the other races have build their communities on TEGs and a newer version of the ancient technologies and energy systems, developed through long processes resembling the post-timeline settings of the LPU, as well as reconnecting to the central sun (Source), the DE2D6 Sirian B crystalline communities, including areas of the DE2D4 and DE2D6, have gone all the way and generated a degree of artificial genetics that can only be seen as unprecedented.

But this is not the whole reason: the differences in opinions are also based upon what is the best development scheme to take for the LPU energy systems and genetics, and this debate is rooted in the predisposed genetics, i.e. the ones with the merged-in TEGs which

142

had a tendency to break down, and what gave rise to the dark ones to take over to begin with.

Beside the fact that the crystalline Sirian Bs are able to transform all infected energy systems and dark TEGs with the crystalline technologies, they are also able to take over whole reality fields and take them out of the evolutionary schemes that for all means and purposes are in the less-progressive universe.

If the Sirian Bs get it their way, there will be no further evolution, no need for viable genetics or new versions of the TEG; all they need is room to move and lots of it to unfold their crystalline communities. The DE2D6 Sirian B crystalline races are consequently posing a threat to both the new stellar races and the ancient stellar races.

The Crystalline Sirian B Solutions
In opposition to the long processes of breeding out the predisposed genetics, some of the Sirian Bs lineage races discovered that a type of crystalline technology could beat the infection in a fast and easy way. The crystalline technology is actually the re-inverted version of the light coding reversal technology utilized by the dark ones, altering the progression fields of the holographic set up. Instead of manipulating the light coding of the settings by reversing the quantum flux fields into steady state fields, where no genetics can evolve, the crystalline Sirian Bs (the CSBs) have taken the light coding of the energy system, based upon the same holographic set up as the reality fields, and utilized the reversal technology here.

This means that the quantum morphogenetic field of the energy system becomes a steady state field with unchanging settings, unable to change according to the surrounding energies of the reality fields. By this the CSBs could beat the infected genetics by reversing the properties of their energy systems and the interconnected reality fields to be unresponsive to the predisposed genetics.

However since their reality fields changed into steady state fields with no quantum flux potentials, a new type of energies have been chosen as the preferred light coding. This light coding is generating the silicate organic form.

To fit the new organic material and the steady state dimensions, running on a specific range of holographic light coding, a template holding a specific number of TEGs (strands) have been evolved. All depending on the scalar fields, i.e. the steady state fields of each sub-field of the crystalline DE2D6 areas, the individual template and its energy system unfold into the silicate organic form, based upon 5-12 strands in the template. In this way the silicate template determine the organic form and the level of intelligence, as in what type of function they are to have and the function of the sub-field. In the CSB communities there are no free evolution or individual chosen function. All is decided beforehand and the organic forms are generated and placed into their respective steady state fields.

This technology has taken time to develop and the first examples and the malfunctioning templates and the energy systems have been dumped on our planet for a long time.[106] The same goes for the early versions of the CSB energy systems that got the infection or had TEGs that began to break down.

Whereas the CSBs are able to freeze in the predisposed genetics, and do so, the non-crystalline races have other solutions to the LPU energy systems and genetics.

---

[106] At some point the middle DE1D3 areas became a place to dump malfunctioning energy systems for all of the experimenting new stellar races. Our reality field then both housed the malfunctioning energy systems and the ones being utilized to solve the issues of the new stellar races. The malfunctioning energy systems were then sealed off and left to burn out inside the reincarnation cycles.

Summing up

To sum up the players having worked together or loosely together, to free the DE1D3 from the dark reign, the non-crystalline DE2D4 and the DE2D5 stellar races have teamed up to free their reality fields from the dark ones and the draco-reptilian overlords (the latter mostly by natural evolution). In spite of the good intentions behind their partnership the agreements, they made to keep this alliance, are being violated, which obviously make the alliance a somewhat unstable one. Nevertheless the unstable alliance prevents the crystalline Sirian Bs (the CSB races) from taking over the rest of the DE2D4, DE2D5 and part of the DE2D6 areas of the LPU, where the new stellar races live.

Most of the CSB races within the DE2D4 and DE2D6 have teamed up under the Guardian Alliance promoting the crystalline agenda. This means that stellar races, holding avian or mammal genetics with a low level of reptoid genetics, have joined the GA and their crystalline worlds.

Mammal races holding a higher degree of reptoid or insectoid genetics have created communities outside the CSB reality fields or have shifted into a sort of exile within the DE1D3 insectoid or DE2D5 reptoid reality fields. Some of the non-crystalline DE2D4 avian and DE2D6 mammal races are collaborating with the HM negotiating on how to return to the HMDE3 Sirian A areas and are taking part in the programs of the future, where time-travel becomes a huge part of the attempts to prevent the crystalline Sirian B agenda from taking over this and other reality fields. It all begins with the time period we are entering now.

The videos *the Sirian B-Reptoid Wars* have to be seen as well to supplement the overview.

The Main Players of our Future

To fully understand what is going on, and why the different factions operate as they do, we have to look into the future first.

It is anticipated that a pole shift is around the corner, if humanity continue the present course and do not modify their consciousness. Here I am talking about the ones being able to do so.[107] Modifying their consciousness means to separate the psyche from the astral barrier. The pole shift will be a direct effect of the fact that the astral barrier is wearing out the 12 pillars keeping the quantum flux field stable. If humanity as a whole, that means including the ones with functional level one energy systems, keep adding more reversed light coding to the barrier, the 12 pillars will collapse.

If the pillars collapse there will be no stellar technology keeping the quantum flux fields stable and the holographic fields will return to the original quantum flux state,[108] which is what we will perceive as a pole shift.

Our planet, before the crystal pillars were inserted, was extremely changeable with an unstable crust, extreme weather and pole shifts that happened more or less every second year. The magnetic field was thin and the planet was a rocky place due to incoming cosmic radiation. Because of this our planet was not, in the period after the timeline event, a place where lifeforms could live in spite of the blueprint of humanoids etc in the gridworks. Naturally the steady

---

[107] The ones with viable level one energy systems have to wake up and take on the responsibility to instigate the needed changes simply because we are the only ones able to do so. We cannot blame the clones or the burned out 4 billion people for not changing since they are literally unable to do so.

[108] Read about why that this in the chapter on Dimensional Bridges in the DE1D3.

state mode from the enclosure is not wished for either and the dark technologies behind this have to go (and with it the electromagnetic energies), but the original 12 pillars are an imperative for a stable middle DE1D3 area with an unwavering surface and an unchangeable holographic field.

The estimate for a pole shift is set to unfold in the period between the years 2045 to 2055, perhaps later. The programs of the different stellar factions, that are unfolding now, are all focused on the surviving landmasses after the anticipated flooding and earthquakes, superfires and other mass destruction. The only landmasses that will stand after the pole shift are the ones with active dimensional bridges and it is here the stellar agendas come in.

The upcoming *true earth humanoids*, the ones taking part in the Sirian A and Maia-Pleiadian DE1D3 humanoid programs, by choosing to stay and become part of the Hyperborean Isle, will unfold in the middle DE3D3 areas as planned. Perhaps many years later than anticipated but it will happen because of the resetting, which for us has been a long awaited opportunity to continue the 5th evolutionary cycle as it was supposed to before the draco-reptilian overlords and then the dark ones took over the DE1D3 reality fields.

The New Stellar-Earth Humanity (the NSEH)
Today a segment of the European enlightened brothers, the DE2D6 Minotaurian masters and their American Illuminati brothers have teamed up with the some of the non-crystalline DE2D4 and DE2D5 new stellar races from the later generations of the avian-reptoid-mammal races as well as the new generations of the Sirian B reptoid-mammal Aryan-Shivas.

Together with the descendants of the draco-reptilian warlords and the remaining Draconians, they have created a state of the art scientific-militant division using technologies from the DE2D5 and DE2D6 areas as well as technologies from races in faraway galaxies.

They have positioned themselves deep down in the North Atlantic Ocean some place between America and England, having created a massive city there called *the New Capitol*. The New Capitol is literally seen as the Ark of NOA, which is fittingly the acronym of *the New Order of the Ages* having been taken to the next level.

First and foremost the NSEH and NOA coalition are working to create the next level of humanity being able to access the dimensions linked up to the outer DE1D3 areas through genetic recognition or via the dimensional bridges, also using genetic recognition. This program is called *the new stellar-earth humanity*, which is why I call the program and the ones performing it the NSEHs.

The NSEHs and NOA are in addition working with plans of taking over the control of America and Europe, with the goal of shutting out the OWO from the Middle East as well as Europe and finally get the full dominion of these areas. But it does not stop there: the NSEH and NOA coalition is working to secure that the DE2D5 new generation of the Maldakian settlers, i.e. the reptoid Nordics, which are supporting the Russians, are not getting a stronghold over Europe through either diplomacy, political plots or by achieving the main control over gold, oil and gas reserves. This is important since the Nordics have teamed up with the lizard Orion Collective controlling the Chinese and most of the Japanese areas (and the dimensional bridges positioned there) and if Russia, China and Japan team up politically and economically as well as sharing stellar technologies and give each other access to the dimensional bridges in their areas, it could easily lead them into a position of world dominion. But this is not all of it, since the NSEH and NOA coalition is also fighting the crystalline Sirian Bs (the CSBs) who are working to take over landmasses from within, using humanity as their allies. The CSBs have already got their crystalline paws on parts of Britain, parts of Scandinavia (all of Finland collaborate with the Nordics. Some parts of Norway and Sweden collaborate with the NSEH and NOA; the rest with the CSBs), South America, parts of southern America, some parts of the Africa, some parts of Australia (the Maia-Pleiadians are preparing to wrest away the power from the CSBs through economical means) and a huge chunk of the South Pole.

For this reason the NSEH and NOA coalition call themselves *the human*[109] *resistance movement* as in going against the reptoid races, incl. the OWO, working to control humanity as in viewing humanity as a servile race. The NSEH and NOA coalition feels that Russia, China, Japan and the rest of the world are selling out their freedom in order to gain stellar technologies. The stellar technologies are not utilized for further progress of humanity but are solely utilized to ensure that the political stakeholders and others with power and money are able to shift out before the pole shift. The fight is also against the Sirian Bs, which are enforcing the crystalline agenda on non-crystalline races by manipulative methods. The NSEH and NOA coalition do not agree with any of these plans. They want to create an upgraded humanity that are able to take over the middle DE1D3 areas after the pole shift as well as overpower the outer DE1D3 areas, creating new colonies in the solar system; first on Mars and later on the other planets.

As I wrote in a newsletter, updated to the new information in this book:

We have much to learn about NSEH and their collaborating new stellar races as well as certain factions of what we understand to be the "Nazis." The Nazi factions we usually are confronted with are the visible ones from the old allies under Hitler[110] *and the avian-reptoid*

---

[109] Earth humanity is a reptoid-mammal race.
[110] Hitler is often seen as a dark one; however he was actually not a dark one to begin with, but held high levels of TEGs that began to break down during his stay. Because

Aldebarans. This old-fashioned conception of what a Nazi is does not seize up to today's terminology as we understood in the video the Shivas, the Aryans and the Nazis. No, the new kids on the block are much more advanced and stem from a pure strain of reptoid genetics fuelled up with second generation Sirian B mammal TEGs. These are the Shiva-Aryans and the new movement collaborating with the US Military division that is part of the NSEH. The old dark-brown militant draco warlords are still present, but they are changing into the next generation and thus new ways of perceiving their stronghold over the US. The goal of the NSEH and NOA is to unfold their post-pole shift world, which will surface from a huge facility beneath the surface of the North Atlantic Ocean after the pole shift. A huge complex that has been build since the 1950's based upon the same technology used in the construction of the ISS which is the equivalent in space arranged by the same forces behind the NSEH and NOA. Naturally the huge underwater complex has met the obstacles of water pressure and similar things by the use of stellar technology. The underwater complex is the New Capitol and the main center for the NSEH and NOA and their stellar allies, i.e. the DE2D5 new stellar races, the Grays, the dark-brown militant Dracos, the Aryans and their "Shiva leaders" (i.e. the original ancient reptoid race). The NSEH and NOA are not planning to eradicate humanity – they are using the mean time to experiment on a humanity 2.0 and helping the geomagnetic pole shift along with different types of sound frequency technologies creating earth quakes and other tectonic movements, forcing the pole shift to accelerate to their convenience. The pole shift will come either way due to the dismantling of the crystal pillar technology creating the environment on our planet by keeping the poles, the magnetosphere and the ionosphere stable.

---

of this he resembles a dark one. Naturally he returned to the dark areas after his stay due to the non-reparable TEGs he had in his level one energy system.

The Religious Beliefsystems

The NSEH and NOA coalition have no intentions in creating religious beliefsystems based upon the old agendas of the OWO. But in the future, semi-religious beliefsystems on Earth and Mars will come in handy to systematize humanity because humans are conditioned to accept a supreme power. Without the gathering under one ruling principle, humanity will not follow the leaders of the post-pole shift world. There has to be some sort of link back to the Old Testament, the deluge and the chosen few, which are to continue the world in a selected and improved form. Thus the religious movement of the NSEH and the NOA coalition is created to entail all religions and fuse them into one, where "we are all worshipping the same supreme power, i.e. Source. Any differences in expression and notion of Source are based upon culturally variation, but in fact we are all worshipping the same creator" just as it was attempted under the reign of Alexander 323 BCE.

The post-pole shift Earth and the humanity 2.0 future, the NSEH and NOA coalition is working to fulfill, is based upon community structures of the new stellar races, they work with, albeit adjusted to the next level of humanity having got the correct gene pool making them prone to a *scientifically based religion*. This combination will ensure that no one is going against the leaders that all will be a representative and refer to Source, of which all humans are all linked together as a unity.

On Mars the leaders will be worshipped as representing Source via the deity we actually see active today, i.e. the Ra entity or the Council of Nine, being the higher dimensional representatives of this entity.[111]

---

[111] There are many other versions of the same theme based upon Egyptian thought forms and ancient stellar races ideologies. None of them stem from actual entities but are being channeled from a holographic program generated to alter the avian genetics.

The teachings of Ra are being implemented, and have since the 1980'ties, into humans that are prepped to transfer to the host-fields leading them to Mars. The humans following the teachings of Ra are undergoing genetically alterations to fit their new lives on Mars. The present day human forefront of Ra will become the new priesthood on Mars. None of the transferred humans will remember having been humans on this planet, given that they are not shifting before after they have shed off the DE1D3 organic form.

The teachings of Ra are resetting the DE2D4 genetics in the level one energy system to accommodate the reality fields of Mars.

Humans connecting to the beliefsystems of Ra are undergoing a slow pre-pole shift transformation process, which is part of the NSEH and NOA coalition plans for the humans that will colonize Mars. The idea of Mars having pyramids are part of a seeding of thoughtforms to attract the needed energies from the astral barrier to work with the genetics in this way and to plant ideas of civilizations being able to live on Mars.

Only when an idea, as a thoughtform, is planted into the collective consciousness field of the ones taking part of that timeline, generating a sub-reality field, will the main reality field reflect back and give it energy. An idea needs energy from the gridworks to be able to manifest. The reality on Mars will be somewhat different from the ancient Egyptian settlements, but there will be glass pyramids and the cities on the surface will be extremely beautiful and attract many DE2D4 races. Beneath in the huge laboratories, a whole other story is being told that has to do with future wars taking place in the solar system and event-lines, which make Star Trek seem inconsequential in comparison.[112] The NSEH and NOA coalition along with their stellar allies are working on the plan on how to take back the quadrant from

---

[112] Star Trek and Star Wars were planted thoughtforms to adjust humanity into preparing for the huge shift into the future.

the crystalline races, the reptoid Maldakian races and the Orion Collective.

The Political Structure

The interstellar political system is based upon trade of knowledge and technology. Along with the trade of technology is trade of genetics given that the genetics are the ones that make the technology work.

TEGs are a major part of this trade of technology. Most modern inventions of stellar technology are linked up to TEGs and the enhancement they hold to be able to attach to different types of light coding, stemming from the many reality fields this quadrant consists of. The TEGs are the foundation of most stellar communities today.

Political leaders are groomed to hold specific abilities which make them fine diplomats and partakers of the supreme councils in this quadrant. The interstellar politics are unfolded in the supreme councils and not internally on the planets (small areas of the main reality fields). The main decisions are made in the supreme council of the main reality field, i.e. a stellar or galactic system.

The interstellar political model is unfolded in both the crystalline and the non-crystalline worlds, in view of the fact that the interstellar political model of the supreme councils and the minor planetary councils, are a remnant from the ancient stellar races living in this quadrant. Another interstellar political model has not been evolved since the ancient stellar races and their idea of a supreme council, where all of the species of the quadrant attend and debate the long term evolution for the quadrant in general, has proven to be the best way to progress as a unit. Whatever is agreed upon in the supreme councils is then taken back to the local or planetary councils. The interstellar politicians are in direct telepathic contact with the supreme councils they belong to and the meetings of all assemblies, given that there is no time. Consequently a council meeting is always in process or can be connected to by the use of genetic time-reversal.[113] The local councils are put to manifest and implement what was instigated on the supreme council meetings. Hence interstellar human politicians are groomed to be able to attend the supreme council meetings and exercise what have been decided into the local councils and the communities the post-pole shift Earth will consist of.

The Societal Structure on Earth

The communities of the post-pole shift humans 2.0 are a combination of the new stellar communities and the structure the NSEH and NOA coalition wants to unfold housing their altered humans. It cannot be fully stellar due to the fact that humans 2.0 hold the genetics of the earth reptoid-mammal humanity in a modified form. Humanity is not able to link up to the technology of the stellar races because humans cannot hold modern TEGs. The stellar races are unable to insert the present day TEGs in humans 2.0 although they have been genetically altered. The new stellar races have undergone an evolution that has taken them genetically away from the earth version of the integrated and biological genetics.

The post-pole shift genetic modification of humanity will be done by action and response systems using thoughtforms and integration of new methods to utilize planetary energies by the means of intellectual recognition through existing beliefsystems and emotional response systems of the psyche. Only when the psyche of the organic form recognizes the value of a teaching, based upon genetic resonance on the radiation level, is the mind able to integrate the new teachings. To enhance the integration process, markers are put

---

[113] Time-reversal is not travelling back in time because there is no time. However there are dissimilar settings of the light coding, which change after each supreme council meeting. Time-reversal is thus going back to the state of the light coding before this or that supreme council meeting and the outcome of it.

in to activate the vibration level of the LPU resonance system.[114] The markers are e.g. strong emotions such as fear, love or the promise of gaining something.

Consequently as the humans shift out of the present organic form, they will enter the next humanity 2.0 on Mars and post-pole shift Earth. Most of them are selected today and in the new incarnational state they will get a genetically modified organic form to house the altered level one energy system and thus are able to hold the TEGs. But that will not happen before one or two generations after the first human 2.0.[115]

The societal structure on Earth and Mars will resemble the stellar communities and their technologies in a modified form and what humans today can think of as the worlds portrayed in science fiction movies. As Earth settles after the pole shift, the colonies on Mars will then have been in play for about 10 to 20 years, the New Capitol will rise from the Ocean floor as the Ark of NOA. From here all political decisions are made. The areas holding functional cities and humans will be come under the control of NSEH and NOA. Supersoldiers, not as in human strength but by exceedingly cultivated psychic abilities and activated level one energy systems, are inserted into these areas holding "normal" humans providing them with the understanding of what they can become. Massive migrations are then set off to the New Capitol and the labs with the goal of altering the surviving humanity into the NSEH model. Most of these humans will die in the process given that the alteration is done technologically and not by the ancient methods of adjusting the DE1D3 energy system back to its original purpose. However the ones that do survive the treatment will establish the next generations of humanity. New societies, built upon

---

[114] More on the LPU resonance system in year two.
[115] Many of the abductions that are not focused on harvesting eggs and sperm (to generate the form of the human 2.0) are done to alter the level one energy system.

stellar technology, will be set up for the ones having completed the treatment, although they are dependent on the chemical and technological components from the New Capitol keeping their modified body and mind intact. Hence all societal structures will be built upon interdependency with the New Capitol, and the NSEH and the NOA leaders.

The Modified Future Humans

The Shiva-Aryans are behind the agenda that is unfolding in Europe and certain parts of the US, i.e. the contributors to the new stellar-earth humanity. But what type of humans is engineered to populate the next world? There are two main factors contributing:

1) Trans-organic and trans-genetic features
2) Human 2.0 based upon pure reptoid genetics

The trans-genetic plan revolves around stellar technologies inserted into the present organic body as well as using the original purpose of the two energy systems, i.e. the LPU holographic energy system and the DE1D3 energy system. It can be hard to accept that the present organic body is sort of an organic android. It has been engineered, bred and transformed into what it is today, based on integrated and biological genetics inserted in a specific ratio to ensure the best functionality of the body for the various experiments and scientific purposes, such as genetic growth and unfolding of new TEGs.

The evidence is seen in the possibilities of genetic mapping, after the genetic code was cracked and understood. Many forms of artificially grown body-parts are on their way by the use of 3D printing, where engineered organic material is used to generate organs etc. The problems with the rejection of a new organ have been solved by the DNA technologies, which take stem-cells and similar materials and from here produce the organic substances to form a new limb, organ, skin or attachment such as noses, ears, faces etc. The 3D printer then forms the appendix.

Trans-organic features will become normal in the future humanity as healthcare issues are solved by purchasing new organs etc. The new earth-stellar humanity will not only hold engineered appendixes and organs; this is just the beginning to adjust the human mind to these features, but also become biologically modified into holding features we today perceive to be "superhuman powers" and abilities.

The advancement in human capabilities is performed by biological engineering using the reptoid genetics to unfold these superhuman powers and abilities. On top of this it will become natural to purchase genetic alterations when first it is scientifically understood how the template and the level one energy system functions in humans.

From here humans will voluntarily re-engineer themselves by going to the alteration stations in the New Capitol, where this is done for a small amount of the new currency; information and trade of genetics. The trade of genetics is normal among stellar races and our DE1D3 area has played a huge role in this, being the alteration station producing genetics that could be healed (self-repair by the use of the genetics in the template), restored (re-generation of the genetics through the DE1D3 energy system) as well as being regenerated (re-built from a fragment of the original genetics).

The new stellar-earth human will understand the "power" and ability to do these three things and the next world, with the New Capitol in front, will become a future center where the NSEH trade this ability to other stellar races in exchange for advancement of specific organic technologies giving access to e.g. advancement in the capability to process information or produce new substances that can be digested through the use of the DE1D3 energy system. All NSEHs will voluntarily act as incubators, by their own free will or because they are mind-controlled by the Shiva-Aryans and their affiliated Minotaurian masters through the reptoid genetics that granted them so much (naturally with the catch that they can be accessed and by this be manipulated to think, what is needed to think to make this society work). The incubator function will not violate any laws of the supreme councils given that the NSEH will appear to accept this function as the main product of humanity to share with the rest of the stellar communities. All stellar communities have something to trade and genetics will become the main trade from the restored DE1D3 under the Shiva-Aryan races and their affiliated Minotaurian masters, the enlightened brothers (the planetary hierarchy) and other reptoid and reptoid-mammal races being part of this plan for the future NSEHs.

The future humanity will get its freedom to become a stellar-earth human being seen as an equal by the other races, although controlled through the genetics they freely accept to integrate to solve certain health issues and similar problems that will arise after the pole shift. Others have freely accepted the infusion of reptoid genetics to gain more muscle power, strength and virility to prolong their lives and yet others just hold the enhanced reptoid genetics as their main source of life-force.[116] The Shiva-Aryans and affiliated brothers and masters thus unfold a future for NSEHs to become trans-genetic incubators to produce genetics for the other stellar races by their own free will.

To ensure order and to keep up the appearance of a stellar community, they are going to reinstate reptoid-aryan humans, i.e. pure breed reptoid earth-stellar humans 2.0 to manage the DE1D3 reality field, holding the leading positions in the governmental system and societies of the post-pole shift world. The reptoid-aryan humans will take over the position of the lizard landlords, not in acting from

---

[116] Strongly coerced by the humans that have got this infusion beforehand; i.e. the ones that are being selected today.

behind the scenes but upfront as party members of governmental organs etc. The middleclass will become the incubators and thus tradesmen of genetics and there will be no poor or lower class humans. All of this will follow the stellar laws as well as upholding all the rules and regulations of the supreme councils.

The future middleclass NSEH communities are to be positioned in Europe,[117] and although the middleclass do not perceive themselves to be workers, the European communities are actually perceived as genetic factories by the other stellar races, seeing the NSEHs as the workers of these.

The European NSEHs will accept their incubation function as taking part in the greater good for all, doing a service to others by producing genetics for the rest of the stellar communities, assisting them in the progress of all evolutions. The NSEHs believe in that they are an important piece of the puzzle and their contribution to the other stellar races are essential for the survival of these races, while they in return become able to enhance their abilities as well as doing well for others. Nonetheless the trans-genetic European humanity is only one part of the future agenda outplayed by the stellar races taking over our reality field.

The Methods of Control

The DE2D4 and DE2D5 races collaborating with the NSEH and NOA use direct methods to activate and lead present day humanity into their grand scheme of how the future is supposed to unfold:

- Energetically generated implants through the means of ray technology, controlling the chakras.

---

[117] Most of North America will perish under the pole shift. Most of the selected humans from the US will therefore become the new population on Mars, whereas the Europeans are to become the new earth-stellar humans.

- Mind-control by the use of inserted reptoid genetics altering the thoughtforms in the mind. E.g. when political leaders are to be elected a broadcast is emitted that affects the reptoid genetics in the throat chakra, making humans vote in the wanted direction.
- Direct interference with the integrated genetics in the level one energy system, via ray technologies.
- Use of DE2D4 and DE2D5 technology to modify the integrated genetics etc.
- Direct intervention in healing sessions, assisting with energy, techniques, sciences of how to work with the energy system behind etc.
- Attempts to "win over" humans that can make a difference according to the political and economical balance between the OWO and the NSEH and NOA future possibilities.
- Manipulation of information producing false Earth history settings, false histories of the origin of humanity etc. supporting the agenda of the intervening stellar humanoid, or group of humanoids and their purpose of being here.
- Attempts to wake up humanity with information that is planted into the web, making humans utilize their reptoid genetics and by this linking up to the thoughtforms they have created in the host-fields.
- Host-fields inserted into the middle DE1D3 areas producing timelines supporting the new thoughtforms with energies, which human accessing the thoughtforms, will be integrating.

Present day humanity is being used to the convenience of the NSEH and NOA coalition. Information is given telepathically to support their ground crew, often inserted DE2D5 new stellar races into human bodies. Many of these are being taken up to crafts during night time to undergo alterations or are transferred to the underwater science labs for adjustments. Human with genetic abilities are taking part in the same programs. Humans that are not part of the genetic enhancement programs are taken too, albeit viewed as lab rats and are treated accordingly.

The goal is to change humanity into a new and better version and the motto is: "some has to die, to enable others to survive."

As with the new stellar races, the trend of genetic assorting or breeding on the ones that hold the correct version of possibilities and genetics, is found in the NSEH and NOA coalition ideas as well.

It is due to this agenda, that I call them the stellar version of the Nazis, beside when I was in contact with the Shiva-Aryans, they themselves called their agenda a modern day Nazi ideology. In this lies a lot of information regarding the first Nazi ideology under the stellar races from Aldebaran, which we only know a minimal portion of.[118]

The Transit Period from the OWO to the NSEH

There will be a period of time, from 2015 and until an unspecific date in 2025 where we shift from the old paradigm into the new, and the forces behind the NSEH and NOA agenda have teamed up with their European allies to make this happen.

The goals are as follows:

1. To merge US and Europe into one 5D dimensional time-zone.
2. To infuse selected Europeans and selected US citizens with a higher level of reptoid genetics making them susceptible to the mind-control broadcasts and subliminal programming.

---

[118] What we do know is that the morphogenetic field behind the Jewish people holds genetic material of the avian-mammal races, stemming back to some of the ancient races of the OWO, i.e. the priestly races. History will be re-written one day where we will understand the true meaning behind the hunting down of the Jews.

3. The goal is to support the NSEH and NOA religious, political and scientific programs by subliminal control.[119]
4. Reinstating reptoid-mammal or avian-reptoid humanoids[120] as leaders and politicians in Europe and US.
5. Pointing at Jeb Bush as president. Jeb has a hybridized type of genetics generated for the purpose. Hilary and Merkel are from the OWO and work together on a subconscious level.
6. Taking out Hollander in France, probably by sexual scandal, and instating another reptoid-mammal leader.
7. Taking out Merkel and take over Germany.
8. Reinforcing NATO to a new level to prepare for possible enforcement against Russia, China and the OWO avian-reptoid factions of the Middle East.
9. Alterations within the EU collaborations and parliament into a more technological oriented organ being less focused upon economy. The goal is to ensure scientific solutions to health issues, medical care, climate and societal issues solving the present challenges within these areas with technology.
10. Allowing private contractors to take over issues that usually are under the governments. The private contractors are to enforce all scientific progress by solving the present crisis of humanity through inventions.

---

[119] E.g. here the Minotaurian masters enter the scene since they are the master-minds of persuasion and subliminal conditioning through the use of the astral barrier as well as the use of how to connect genetically to the throat chakras of the selected humans with the higher level of reptoid genetics. Again we remember that reptoids are human-like and not the regressed reptilians.

[120] Some of the old bloodlines of avian-reptoid controllers, i.e. the lizards, are collaborating with the NSEH and NOA coalition. As part of the agreements these lizards are re-instated into their former positions of power and money.

The Moon

The Moon will keep its function as a transit area for the many stellar races that will enter our solar system in the future. Preparations are being made for this by installing stellar technologies and docking stations run by earth humans of our present type, although slightly altered to be able to exist on the Moon, in collaboration with DE2D4 and DE2D5 new stellar races taking part of these projects. Thus the Moon is being lifted into the next stage as a team-work between all factions wanting to become a part of the reset DE1D3 reality field.

The reset DE1D3 reality field is understood to be the solar system after it has undergone the resetting altering the present system back to the settings the DE1D3 reality field was engineered to hold by the creators of the DE1D3. The solar system has already undergone its resetting and it is only because of the astral barrier that we cannot see it. The European and American enlightened brothers and their human affiliates have already positioned themselves on the Moon where a thriving community is part of the stellar communities having lunar stations positioned there.

The Moon is not just a planetoid, but engineered control station where all stellar races transit in and out of our solar system. The Moon is a vital part of the reset DE1D3 reality field, being the transit area to enter and leave the system from the other dimensions. The Moon holds higher dimensional energies by the use of *dimensional accelerators*.

Dimensional accelerators are huge energy beams that generate a dimensional bridge into which crafts from other dimensions can produce a holographic field where they are able to manifest as 4th or 5th dimensional matter.

These fields can be stretched into the facilities on the back side of the Moon and by this all stellar races can enter and be part of the transit areas without undergoing any dimensional alternation or

163

dimension down-grading to be able to communicate with the earth human scientists and other dimensional humanoids present there.

Regarding the Shiva-Aryans, they exist in the DE2D6 vicinity and are not part of our reality field and will not become part of it. They visit from time to time in their huge plasma crafts to ensure that the project and their inserted genetics are doing well – they see this as an investment. The plasma crafts oscillate in the 4th dimension and cannot go lower in dimensionality. Thus the Moon is their preferred place, when they visit our reality field.

Other Minor Players
There are other minor players active inside and outside the barrier, having their own genetic programs to unfold, e.g. the Gray-Sirian B insectoid-reptoid *Novo Sapiens programs.* There is also the humanoid looking Gray type of body, i.e. *the hybrid programs*, mostly done by the Grays alone. None of these programs are to be seeded into this reality field, but are put in other systems of the DE2D4 and DE2D5 reptoid areas. Most of the Gray hybrid programs are coming to an end, since they have achieved what they came here to do in the late 1950's. They have breed their new type of Gray-humanoid body from the genetics in sealed off level one energy systems and human biological genetics. Thus there is no need to go further into this.

The crystalline Sirian Bs also have their genetics programs of an *8 stranded earth human* instigated to become their worker collective in the reset DE1D3 system, after their grand takeover. The 8 stranded human will not be able to evolve beyond the 8 strands given the fact, that these strands are engineered and based upon crystalline TEGs.

The CSBs have the custom to breed their version of the indigenous humanoids in the reality fields they control. In that way they honor the present inhabitants and their genetics, albeit in the form, they prefer.

164

The goal is to produce subservient humanoids accepting the CSBs as their leaders, even though they are not present in any of the reality field they control and are far away in the DE2D6. The engineered crystalline TEGs ensure this.

As with all of the other CSB controlled races, the TEG controlled humanoids are linked up to *a soul matrix* as they call it. The soul matrix is the main principle of all of the crystalline TEGs fueling them with the needed light coding to keep them functional. The soul matrix works as a substitution for the central sun. As such the TEG controlled crystalline races are working as a unity, or a hive mind via the soul matrices. Hence there is no possibility for breaking out or go into an individual progression. When a humanoid has become part of the CSBs, the humanoid is altered and linked up to the soul matrix. From there, there is no point of return.

The plus side is that the crystalline humanoid stays as it is forever and ever, never breaking down, unless the soul matrix is dissolved. The dissolving of a soul matrix happens when the leading CSBs decide that this type of humanoid has to be taken out of production due to lack of functionality.

The Benevolent Players of our Future

Before we move on, a little understanding has to be made. Up until now I have talked about the DE3 areas as unspecified, or as holding the 7-9th dimension. However due to new Sirian A engineered TEGs, the descendants of the Sirian A lineages have been able to create sub-field within the areas of non-distorted DE3. These areas hold the 4-6th dimensions to accommodate the stellar races from the DE2 systems who want to join the progression programs back to the HM through the Sirian A bridge zones since these are the last bridge zones which are fully intact. These DE3 lower dimensions are utilized as areas of genetic progression, schooling and adjusting to the true DE3 vibration and radiation levels.

The Benevolent DE3D4 GFOL

Different stellar races are part of the new DE3 areas outside the DE2 systems. These races are benevolent and their areas border up to the DE2D4 areas and the outer DE1D3 areas.

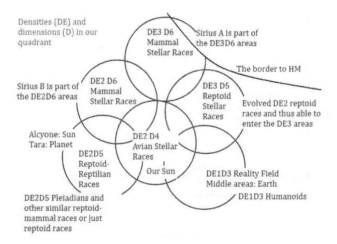

Densities (DE) and dimensions (D) in our quadrant

DE3 D6 Mammal Stellar Races

Sirius A is part of the DE3D6 areas

The border to HM

Sirius B is part of the DE2D6 areas

DE2 D6 Mammal Stellar Races

DE3 D5 Reptoid Stellar Races

Evolved DE2 reptoid races and thus able to enter the DE3 areas

Alcyone: Sun
Tara: Planet

DE2 D4 Avian Stellar Races

DE2D5 Reptoid-Reptilian Races

Our Sun

DE1D3 Reality Field Middle areas: Earth

DE2D5 Pleiadians and other similar reptoid-mammal races or just reptoid races

DE1D3 Humanoids

To accommodate the need of the DE2D4 avian races, which are willing and ready to return to the HM, the races of the DE3D4 areas work together under *the Galactic Federation of Light* (and no; it is not the ones we hear of on the internet). The true Galactic Federation of Light (the GFOL) is a scientific project instigated by *the DE3D6 stellar races descending from the first DE3 Sirian As*, concentrating on turning the DE2D4 avian brothers and sisters into legal participants of the DE3D4 galactic councils to ensure them the technologies and knowledge on how to reconnect to the holographic metaverse. Many of the DE2 races view the DE3D4 and DE3D5 galactic races to be their teachers and mentors.[121] The true Galactic Federation of Light is a collective created to assist the many species of the DE3D4 areas. Some of the participants of the GFOL are from the DE2D4 and DE2D5 areas where they had avian-reptoid-mammal genetics, and they have all undergone the transition from DE2D4 or DE2D5 to DE2D6.

Many of the new stellar races do not care for the original ways of progression and the GFOL advocate for these ways of progression by the use of the original methods modified to be able to work with the altered genetics in their DE2D4 siblings.

The goal of the GFOL is to activate the original ways of progression in all stellar races and by this ensure that they can, if they want, return to the holographic metaverse. The GFOL thus holds knowledge of the holographic metaverse and the fact that the DE2s and DE3s have LPRF races positioned in the higher areas of the LPU, stemming from the first races and that they generated the central sun. However the GFOL are often viewed as the enemy of the new stellar races unfolding the TEG technologies to their fullest and many negative attributes have been given to the GFOL across the DE2 areas. Inside the enclosure the GFOL have been imitated by other reptoid-mammal

---

[121] When you are under the control of the DE2D5 manipulation, the original DE3 races appear to be something we are to fear and shone away from.

humanoids, presenting themselves as the Asthar Command and the archangels, using the language of the GFOL as their way in. *Asthar and his archangels* are renegade reptoids holding a lineage back to the Maldakian reptoid settlers. After the timeline event the LPRF3 Maldak was blown apart, and as we know this generated the Moon in the DE1D3; however parts of the gridwork from the LPRF3 Maldak settlements created the foundation of the DE2D5 Pleiadian system, where the DE2D5 ancient stellar races created new settlements. Not all of the ancient DE2D5 Pleiadians regressed into the reptilians.[122] However a group of the non-regressed ancient Pleiadians took part in the Reptilian Riots and this group goes under the name of Asthar and his archangels. Asthar and his archangels were excluded from the Pleiadian communities shortly after the riots (before the full DE2D5 fell under the dominion of the overlords) due to their unfaithful alliances with the draco-reptilian warlords. This faction of ancient Pleiadian reptoids were condemned for their war crimes against the reptoid races and were left to their own, only having their warships to live in. One of their warships is called Pegasus and the leader of this is Asthar, the shiny one.

The language of Asthar and the DE2D5 renegade reptoids are strongly militaristic since they are warriors and have for eons existed on their warships having no system to return to. During the dark reign they were allowed to settle on the Moon, and many of them became affiliated with the LWBs of the OWO. The archangels are thus in cahoots with the LWBs controlling the enclosure. Hence the renegade reptoids know the terminology of the LWB false teachings and the like, imposing to be benevolent forces wanting to evolving humanity.

---

[122] However many of the newer generations of Pleiadians, holding reptoid-mammal genetics have collaborated with the draco-reptilian overlords after the regressed DE2 communities based upon trade etc were formed, either by free will or by having been overtaken by the draco-reptilian overlords.

Asthar and his archangels should be called the Galactic Federation of Darkness. The renegade reptoids are made of organic plasma able to shift from one form into another, more or less like a shape-shifter. The plasma is pale blue-golden. Today they present themselves in an organic guise of the made-up version of the Pleiadians or take on the ascended master imagery generated for the purpose. The true GFOL cannot go lower than the DE3D4 and therefore they are unable to use the dimensional bridges to the DE1D3 reality field.[123] Most of the true GFOL collaborate with the DE2D4 avian races that have not accepted the Sirian B crystalline agenda or the other factions within the new stellar human societies built upon TEGs and stationary organic bodies.

Contrary to most understandings the GFOL are actually considered one of the true allies of the earth humanity and the GFOL have many times attempted to negotiate in the supreme councils the release of the level one energy systems enabling humanity to become the stellar humanoids we once were. Earth humans would pose a strong ally in their scientific attempts to re-gain the original progression abilities where integrated and biological genetics progress naturally – again in their altered less-progressive slow ratio. The GFOL are negotiating with the DE2D4 RWB that remained in Europe, offering solutions to re-generate the genetics the RWBs lost, as well as figuring out solutions to remove the dark separation technologies inserted into them.

The DE3D4 Races and the DE2D4 Avian Host-fields

To solve the problem of transfer from the DE1D3 to the DE3D4 avian and to some degree reptoid and mammal communities, host-fields have been installed to generate a genetic bridge from the outer DE1D3 areas bordering up the benevolent DE2D4 avian-mammal

---

[123] Thus humans cannot contact the true GFOL and they cannot contact humans.

areas.[124] The avian-mammal DE2D4 areas are participating in this collaboration, acting as the host-field energetically, since they are working with their DE3D4 brothers and sisters. However the host-fields can only be utilized by humanoids with the correct genetic DE2D4 or TEG infused DE3D4 combination matching the DE2D4 areas, they have to pass through. How to get there can only be given to the ones, who are able to telepathically connect on their own to the assisting crafts placed in the vicinity of the DE1D3 areas in the dimensional cross-zones between reality fields.

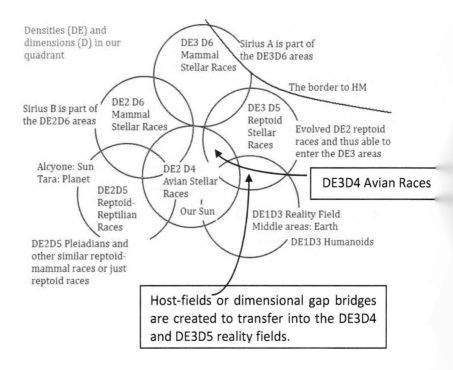

Densities (DE) and dimensions (D) in our quadrant

DE3 D6 Mammal Stellar Races

Sirius A is part of the DE3D6 areas

The border to HM

Sirius B is part of the DE2D6 areas

DE2 D6 Mammal Stellar Races

DE3 D5 Reptoid Stellar Races

Evolved DE2 reptoid races and thus able to enter the DE3 areas

Alcyone: Sun
Tara: Planet

DE2D5 Reptoid-Reptilian Races

DE2 D4 Avian Stellar Races

Our Sun

DE3D4 Avian Races

DE1D3 Reality Field Middle areas: Earth

DE1D3 Humanoids

DE2D5 Pleiadians and other similar reptoid-mammal races or just reptoid races

Host-fields or dimensional gap bridges are created to transfer into the DE3D4 and DE3D5 reality fields.

---

[124] Many of present day avians border up to the DE3D6 benevolent areas and thus they hold mammal genetics.

The host-fields cannot be entered in present organic form of humans and they only become visible, when the present biological form has been shed off. This pose a problem to the ones wanting to get to the DE2D4 areas by the bridges and solutions are called for to ensure that the correct information is delivered to the earth humanoids wanting to go through the DE2D4 progression fields to the DE3D4. Most of the original dimensional bridges between the DE1D3 and the DE3 reality fields have been destroyed and thus the host-fields are needed to bridge the dimensional gap of these areas.

The DE2D5 and the Benevolent DE3D5 Solutions

Few stellar races from the DE2D5 areas, i.e. the non-crystalline areas, are advocating in the councils to let the present humanity on earth stay where they are, as those they have become. Some of them are supporting the drop-zone politics whereas others are advocating for a solution to the DE2D5 humanoids that were taken from the ancient areas and brought unwillingly to the enclosure. However due to the pre-deposition of the infection in the ancient DE2D5 genetics, most DE2D5 councils and their new stellar races do not take action to the talk.

In contrast the Maia-Pleiadian races[125] having shifted to the DE3D5 areas, are ready to invite the earth humanoids into their habitats, but only the ones who remember who and what they are. As with the host-fields, the DE3D5 areas cannot be accessed or connected to before earth humanoids lift their genetics to be able to telepathically connect on their own or shed off the present organic form, which is composed of reversed technologies.

---

[125] The Maia-Pleiadians are outside our known list of "Pleiadians". The known Pleiadians are renegade reptoid races and reptilian races having joined the draco-reptilian overlords to participate in the genetic trade and scientific experiments. Present day Pleiadians are collaborating with the LWBs etc.

Therefore dimensional gap bridges have been put between the DE1D3 and the DE3D5 areas using the technologies to accommodate the ability to enter the dimensional gap bridges. However since most of the teachings to this level of activation is part of the second year, I will not go further into it here.

We will be very surprised to see the Maia-Pleiadian humanoid. First and foremost they do not hold physical form, we know of.

A Maia-Pleiadian is around 2m tall, have predominantly silver-white-blue colored skin, big blue eyes, bright golden or white hair, radiate a slight glow of blue-golden light and is able to shift organic body from 5D to 3D by will.

This race predominantly communicates through energy flows into the heart vortex and only with the ones that have mammal genetics and are able to communicate "from center to center of kindness".

They have no language as such, but are visual and energetic telepaths. The old saying: "Only the pure of heart will enter the Kingdom of Heaven" refers to the old pathways of the Silver Star gridwork.

The Maia-Pleiadian are here to lift the "heart and soul" of the ones being ready to truly leave the mindset of human behavior.

They focusing on teachings of kindness, self-empowerment and understanding of what a soul infused human is, i.e. the psychology of the true DE1D3 earth humanoid.

10 Signs that you are encountering a benevolent humanoid

1. The first greeting will always be telepathic and give rise to a sensation of "something is good here". There will be no doubt.
2. Such races will be polite and greet you in a manner that shows non-hostility and diplomatic intentions (this unfortunately also unfold with the non-benevolent races).
3. True stellar humanoids will hold a high degree of information and knowledge that exceeds normal enclosure information.
4. They will never use the present beliefsystems of the enclosure but try to encourage a new level of understanding by the use of energy and consciousness to activate the potentials we hold.
5. The exchange of information will always be in forms of images and energy sensations directed to the energy system to awake it into activation and the will to progress.
6. The exchange happens directly to the middle and upper centre of the level one energy system (the heart and brain centre) to ensure that the correct pull in of energy from their gridwork is activated.
7. Delivering energy and consciousness is always the first step to peaceful communication and the exchange of energy from the gridwork of the race is showing the origin of the race.
8. Encountering the energies of the gridwork behind the humanoid form will always activate similar genetics in the addressed humanoid from which the genetics are activated and full inner telepathic understanding can be infused.
9. Therefore a true encounter with a stellar humanoid will be of grace, uplifting, leave an imprint of energy and consciousness and the ability to access new levels of information from within.
10. They will always return, because the moment the energetic and genetic connection is in place, the progress of all races will continue.

Overview of Universes and Races

If we are to sketch the divisions and the races they led to into broad strokes, it would unfold like this:

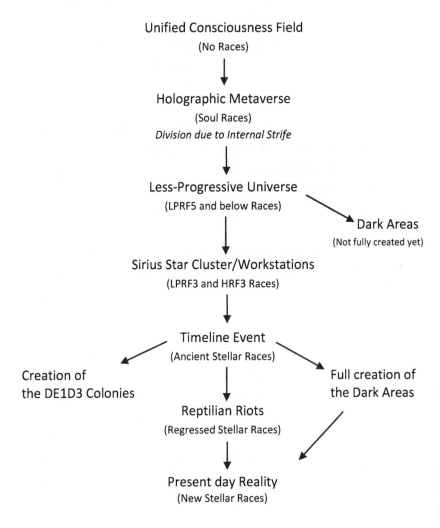

Unified Consciousness Field
(No Races)

Holographic Metaverse
(Soul Races)
Division due to Internal Strife

Less-Progressive Universe
(LPRF5 and below Races)

Dark Areas
(Not fully created yet)

Sirius Star Cluster/Workstations
(LPRF3 and HRF3 Races)

Timeline Event
(Ancient Stellar Races)

Creation of
the DE1D3 Colonies

Full creation of
the Dark Areas

Reptilian Riots
(Regressed Stellar Races)

Present day Reality
(New Stellar Races)

The Races and Their Genetics

The soul races of the holographic metaverse are what we perceive as spiritual races, "consciousness-integrated-into-form-races", i.e. highly developed intelligent and wise soul infused humanoids in full contact with the core principles of their reality fields, also in the lower HRFs.

The soul races consist of an orb with soul genetics merged with holographic light coding generating a changeable and dynamic form fit for *the holographic resonance field* (HRFs) the humanoid wishes to take part of. The form is chosen for the elevation cycle according to the chosen resonance field and the races existing there. Circulation between HRFs is common and as the light coding transform in contact with the soul genetics, the stronger the soul genetics get and the less dense the form becomes. All genetics have to be evolved to their fullest in each elevation cycle before the next cycle can be instigated or entered.

Eventually all HRFs of the HM have been visited - the soul genetics having done their transformational work in the elevation cycles - and the consciousness units can return to the unified consciousness field or become one with the oversoul groups again. There are no densities or dimensions in the HM, only HRFs with various ratios of light coding and soul genetics. The soul races[126] are unable to connect to us unless we activate a higher ratio of functional soul genetics; then they can communicate with us through the soul genetics and instruct us how to return to the HM, where we can continue the true evolution.

---

[126] I have in my earlier material called the soul races for the true humans and the soul genetics for true human genetics. My understanding of the true human genetics is actually not correct.

The soul races are divided into following genetic segments:

- The HRF1 soul races hold insectoid genetics to be unfolded to their fullest in the third elevation cycle.
- The HRF2 soul races are done with the insectoid genetics and now unfold the avian, the reptoid and the mammal genetics. They are actively part of the third elevation cycle, opting to enter the fourth, or are part of the fourth cycle.
- The HRF3 soul races are done with the avian and the reptoid genetics and the fourth elevation cycle. The HRF3s have just about fully developed mammal genetics and they are part of the fifth elevation cycle, developing the genetics needed to enter the sixth elevation cycle, which lead to the major sixth evolutionary cycle.
- The HRF4 soul races have fully developed mammal genetics, have entered the sixth elevation cycle, where the true human genetics are developed and have begun the pre-stages of the major sixth evolutionary cycle.
- The HRF5 soul races have active and functional sixth elevation cycle genetics i.e. true human genetics, and have entered the major sixth evolutionary cycle.

The LPRF5 and below races of the LPU are holographic in nature like the soul races of the holographic metaverse, but their soul genetics are voluntarily added with *the first generation of TEGs* to make them able to connect to the LPU central sun. In the LPRF3 and LPRF2 the TEGs and soul genetics are put into a template and energy system, which is foreign to the soul races. The holographic form consists of a slightly reversed type of light coding, which make them progress in a slower pace. The slow progression was the whole issue of the Internal Strife and divided the soul and less-progressive races into two verses.

176

The LPRF4 and LPRF5 races are benign humanoids from the HM with a high level of soul genetics. They are plasma-like in form and to begin with they resembled the HRF4 and HRF5 races to a high degree. The LPRF4 and LPRF5 races cared for the soul races of the third elevation cycle and therefore ended up generating their own holographic universe to take care of the soul races from the third elevation cycle. Today the LPRF4 and LPRF5 races are less-progressive in nature and hold little resemblance to the original true human, they once were. They founded the less-progressive universe, its reality fields and areas, the template and energy systems and established the foundation of all lifeforms we know of. Although compared to the regressive and new stellar races, they seem benevolent. However they are, in contrast to the holographic metaverse, deflected races holding modifications and the first generation of TEGs. They went against the natural order of things and as such turned their back on the oversoul groups. These races will eventually, as all races inside the less-progression universe, return to the holographic metaverse.

The LPRFs are divided into following genetic segments:
- *The LPRF2s* have higher evolved insectoid and avian genetics, as well as medium levels of reptoid genetics developed in different combinations. They have a higher level of the first generation of TEGs.
- *The LPRF3 races* have higher developed reptoid and medium-developed mammal genetics also added TEGs, but in a lower ratio.
- *The LPRF4 races* have fully developed mammal genetics and very small amounts of TEGs.
- *The LPRF5s* have almost none TEGs and they have kept their soul genetics from the HM.

The ancient stellar races arose after the timeline event, where the mixed core of the Sirius system and the infection led to an explosion, which in turn generated a remodeling of all reality fields of the LPRF3 and LPRF2 areas. The timeline event led to a division inside the LPU between the LPRF4 and LPRF3 of which most of the LPRF3 turned into the DE3 dark areas except a few areas under the now present DE3 Sirian A lineages. The ancient stellar races have *merged-in TEGs and soul genetics*, which is not necessarily their own. All holographic forms were re-shuffled during the timeline event, leading to much confusion to begin with.

The ancient stellar races invented *the second generation of TEGs* to modify the merged-in genetics and by this exceeded the golden ratio of 80% soul genetics and 20% TEGs to a 70-30 ratio. They had to do this to survive the new organic forms as well as the solidified reality fields, which arose after the timeline event in the LPRF3 and LPRF2, producing the foundation of the galaxies in our present day universe. From here the densities and dimensions arose, which is why we after the timeline event get the DE3 races (the 7th, 8th and 9th dimension) and DE2 races (the 4th, 5th and 6th dimension).

The DE1D3 arose as a joint effort between the remaining non-dark LPRF3s and the HMDE3s (HRF3 races who entered the LPU). The DE1D3 reality field and colonies were generated in the DE1D3. The 3rd dimension is not a natural level of existence, albeit the quantum flux fields (the QFFs) it is generated out of are, since the QFFs are the foundation of all densities and not bound by dimensionality.

The Regressive Races began in the DE2D5 areas after the timeline event, where the ancient stellar reptoid races (human-like) regressed into their previous genetics forms of the fourth evolutionary cycle, taking back on the animal form. From here we get the reptilians, the avians and insectoid races. *Third generations of TEGs*, predominantly mammal based, were invented to assist the DE2D5s to return to their ancient stellar settings, but without any larger success. The insertion of the third generation of TEGs diminished the golden ratio further to a 60-40 ratio, some even 50-50, adding to the possibility of breaking down, which became the outcome of many of the regressive DE2D5s, pulling more of this dimension into the dark areas.

This, along with the regression of the merged-in TEGs, set back the whole progressing of the DE2 areas, since the regressive races turned highly violent and selfish. Greed, lust etc arose from the regression. This behavior was not common in the fourth evolutionary cycle, but a new trait stemming from the regressive races and the holographic light coding that came with their existence. The DE2D5 draco-reptilian and their allies amongst the regressive races instigated the Reptilian Riots and wiped out most of the ancient stellar races, in sheer anger and lust for revenge. In their regressed state, they felt abandoned by their peers and by this slaughtered them.

The new stellar races are born out of a mix of the regressed races and their genetic experiments and attempt to regain their prior ancient stellar race status. Others are created as an attempt to upgrade the regressed forms into more human-like forms and similar experiments of which the DE1D3 areas have played a vital role.

Most of the new stellar races are unaware of the LPRF4 and LPRF5 races above their dimensions, since *the repulsion zone* between the DE3 and the LPRF4 prevents them to look higher. They are aware of the dark ones in the DE3, and as such they mostly avoid entering this density field. The highest positioned stellar races live in the DE2D6 under the guardianship of the Sirian B descendants.

Fourth and fifth generations of TEGs have been evolved inside the DE2D6, generating consciousness abilities to higher dimensions and thus created these dimensions from the TEGs.

These higher dimensions are grown out of the regressed areas of the DE2D6 and are as such whole new types of dimensions, with no resemblance to the LPRF4 and LPRF5. Thus our universe is expanding from below, generating a whole new set of dimensions and densities, evolving out of the new stellar races.

It should be duly noted that the DE3 Sirian A have accomplished to generate new dimensions as well in their areas of the DE3; however these are fueled with HM light coding since they have been generated in collaboration with the HRF3s.

The Density Lifeforms

The lifeforms in the densities consist of three dimensions. Some consist of more, depending on the TEGs they have inserted, albeit these layers of multidimensionality are most commonly accessed as consciousness, i.e. as projection of the TEGs (in our dimension rarely as genetics) into other dimensions.

Projection of consciousness happens via the expansion of the radiation field (the upper triangle field) where the genetics/TEGs are able to link up to the dimensions they have been in before, dimmed down to be able to enter a lower dimension or as upgraded TEGs inserted there with the intention of establishing telepathic contact with a specific group in another dimension.

Inserting TEGs in the upper template is often done to gain access as physical presence in a higher dimension aside from the succeeding one following the laws of progression from one dimension to the next. When inserting higher dimensional TEGs, the energy system is able to shift into the higher dimension when the inserted higher dimensional TEGs of the upper template have been integrated into the energy system; e.g. a DE2 energy system can have inserted D6 mammal TEGs in the template, making it possible to jump from the 4D into the 6D, when integrated into the personality and energy system. Some of the DE2s have come into our reality field to be able to do such jumps due to the blueprints in our gridworks.

However most of the time, the attempt to do a dimensional jump demands a very high level of TEGs, and a high level often exceed the golden ratio. Therefore most of the higher dimensional TEGs break down when they are integrated into the energy system, making the energy system decay or at worst, turn into a dark one.

The density lifeforms are for short called DE and the dimensions are named the D3, D4 etc.

The first organic lifeform is what we know as the human body and it consists of three dimensions of which the two are not genuine dimensions compared to the other densities, because in a density one system, the DE1, the 1st and 2nd dimensions are part of the evaporation zones, being pulled into the quantum flux fields, the DE1D3 level of our density, by the decaying energies of the astral barrier.

The energies of the astral barrier are decaying due to the huge section of decomposing energy systems, having been put into the reintegration cycles (the afterlife and reincarnation areas) to slowly burn out, making it possible to harvest the viable genetics of the upper template.

DE1 $\left\{\begin{array}{l} \end{array}\right.$ 1st Dimension or mineral level, i.e. last stage before evaporation

2nd Dimension or the atomic level, i.e. electromagnetic flux

3rd Dimension or the quantum flux fields, i.e. the true 3rd dimension

The density two lifeforms, the DE2s, hold three genuine dimensions, which are part of the post-timeline event areas, i.e. the 4th, 5th and 6th dimensions. Usually a DE2 lifeform holds the organic, or matter body generated of post-timeline light coding in the lowest dimension, the energy system in the middle, holding the already integrated genetics and TEGs, and the genetics and TEGs in the template are positioned in the highest dimension as possibilities to be integrated.

Naturally there are other combinations such as a DE2D4 body, a DE2D4 energy system and DE2D6 genetics added with TEGs, or a DE2D5 body, a DE2D6 energy system and DE2D6 genetics, or a DE2D4 body, a DE2D4 energy system and DE2D5 genetics, etc. The variations can take place because of the TEGs, adding light coding to the system it would be out of reach of in normal circumstances.

DE2
$\left.\begin{array}{l}\text{4}^{th}\text{ Dimension unfolds the DE2 organic form}\\ \text{5}^{th}\text{ Dimension holds the energy system (the DE2HES)}\\ \text{6}^{th}\text{ Dimension holds the genetics in the upper template}\end{array}\right.$

The density three lifeforms, the DE3s, hold three genuine dimensions from the post-timeline event dimensions. The construction is as in the DE2s with different combinations added with TEGs, merged-in or placed there.

DE3
$\left.\begin{array}{l}\text{7}^{th}\text{ Dimension holds the DE3 organic form}\\ \text{8}^{th}\text{ Dimension holds the energy system (the DE3HES)}\\ \text{9}^{th}\text{ Dimension holds the genetics in the upper template}\end{array}\right.$

In contrast to the density matter forms, the HM form consists of three interchangeable versions or levels, where the soul genetics are integrated directly and develop through the various settings of light coding. The HM form was the foundation of the LPU template, energy systems and organic form:

- The HM radiation level gave grounds for the upper template and the radiation field with its light coding in the reality field lifeforms.
- The HM vibration level gave ground for the vibration field and its light coding in the reality field lifeforms, generating the energy system.
- The HM light coding interchangeable form gave ground for the lowest dimension and the organic body of the reality field lifeforms.

These three systems kept their basic form and light coding during the timeline event, but were naturally altered into the more solidified density bodies and the dimensional sub-fields of these.

Therefore when we work with the auric fields in genetic activation in year two, we work with the remnants of the original three layered holographic resonance system, which the soul races still hold in the HM. Thus the first step of undoing the effects of the timeline event is to alter the density system back into is original LPU first form, or pre-timeline event reality field form.

The LPU Holographic Energy System

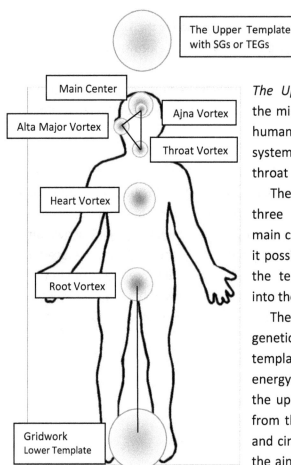

The Upper Template
with SGs or TEGs

Main Center

Ajna Vortex

Alta Major Vortex

Throat Vortex

Heart Vortex

Root Vortex

Gridwork
Lower Template

The Upper Triangle is creating the mind and personality of the humanoid holographic energy system. It consists of the ajna, throat and alta major vortexes.

The energy circulation of the three vortexes generates the main center in the head making it possible for the genetics from the template to be embodied into the vortexes of the system.

The progression ability of the genetics is accumulated in the template and when the correct energy settings are created in the upper triangle, the genetics from the template will descend and circulate the potentials into the ajna, the alta major and the throat vortex connecting the new possibilities to the sense of self in the stellar-humanoid personality.

The Ajna Vortex is connected to the main head center and unfolds the features of perception and understanding of internal and external energies and their interaction with the genetics. If the ajna vortex is harmed in any way, the consciousness principles from the template are unable to connect to the mind of the holographic system and the present form cannot process the information from the other vortexes and the genetics unfolded there.

The Throat Vortex makes the holographic energy system able to process energy internally and externally in a conscious way. The throat vortex holds the main genetics that unfold the "personality".

The Alta Major Vortex enables the ajna and throat vortexes to work consciously with the root vortex. The alta major vortex gives the ability to work with light coding by pulling it in from the gridworks through the root vortex. The energies are unfolded by the use of holographic symbols, geometry and tonal sequences.

The Heart Vortex interacts with the light coding of the previous or present reality field, where the personality and its genetics took on form. If the personality and integrated genetics are activated, it will be from the present reality field it will pull in light coding to sustain the hara quadrant. When the energy circulation needs to be altered, making it possible for new genetics to enter the main head center and from here integrate into the energy system, the vortexes have to change their oscillation. Energetic enhancement is done by altering the light coding of the holographic energy system to make it capable of interfacing with a new level of light coding settings in the reality field, it is part of. This is achieved by conscious activation coming as an incentive from the template being ready to unfold the next level of the genetics into the energy system. Thus genetic activation cannot be forced; only when the possibilities of the previous set of genetics have unfolded to the highest potentials, can the next be integrated.

The Root Vortex is connected to the gridwork, i.e. the foundation of a reality field, where the genetics of the template were created to begin with. The gridwork is linked up to the races and the density the genetics stems from. In our understanding of the template and where the genetics stem from, whether they are created, i.e. technological enhanced genetics (TEGs) or soul genetics, the root vortex will always link the genetics to the density where they were created.

Only when the stellar humanoid with its fully developed genetics is ready to return to the HM will the root vortex dissolve and the genetics begin the process of creating the original consciousness system of the soul (the true light body). The root vortex sustains the LPUHES with light coding from the gridwork making it possible to unfold an organic form. It also holds the quantum morphogenetic blueprint of the body that fits the genetics in the template.

The Upper Template (genetic template)
The upper template holds the soul genetics or the TEGs generated for the purpose of functioning inside the LPU. Most of the genetics are modified to be able to work with the light coding of the gridworks or they are in a dormant state and need to be activated, integrated and developed.

The Lower Template (gridwork template)
The gridwork template is connected to khundarays from the central sun (the artificial core of the LPU) but it also holds storages of light coding from the reality field where it was generated. The gridworks are activated by the genetics in the energy system and the interaction between the energy system, the genetics and the gridwork they are part of, generate a reality. The genetics link up to the timelines in the reality field (sub-fields), where the energy system unfolds its presence or existence. Timelines are both individual and collective.

The New Stellar Races and Their Genetics

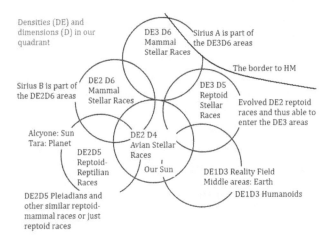

The new stellar races are the descendants of the draco-reptilians and other regressed races that did not team up with the dark ones. The regressed races have since the dark ones came into power attempted to solve the problem of the dark ones and the predisposed genetics.

The non-dark factions of DE2 stellar races teamed up in councils with representatives from the mammal, insectoid, avian and the reptoid communities around the DE2 quadrant, in an effort to create a much stronger lineage of humanoids by altering their genetics to hold a variety of reptoid genetics[127] and genetic combinations of TEGs. Consequently the new stellar races of today all hold variations of the reptoid genetics.[128] The Pleiadians and other DE2D5 humanoids are

---

[127] The reptoid genetics are the strongest and hence the best to build a new energy system from to hold larger quanta of light coding in the energy system. This system is then used as a basis for the other genetics, mostly infused as TEGs or holding fragmented or cloned insectoid, avian and mammal genetics from the races holding the most viable forms of genetics, shared in this effort to circumvent the infection along with the breeding programs.

[128] Which is why the information about the Sirian b-Reptoid Wars becomes important seen in this light.

therefore reptoid-mammal or mammal-reptoid in genetic structure, since they have upgraded their reptoid genetics with mammal TEGs or downgraded their mammal genetics with reptoid infusions. The DE2D4 stellar races have avian-reptoid genetics with insectoid TEGs and other combinations to be able to stand in their light so to speak and withstand the dark ones. Many genetic experiments were instigated to solve the problem of the predisposed genetics with their merged-in TEGs as well as how to avoid getting overshadowed or unwillingly merged with the dark TEGs and the infected genetics in the contact around the quadrant with the races under the stronghold of the dark ones. The races under the dark ones all carry some level or another of the dark TEGs, dark separation technology or have been infected with the dark genetics by allowing the dark ones to overshadow them, i.e. possess their energy systems leaving behind an imprint of the overshadowing dark one (and thus always be to his or her disposal). If the genetics were predisposed to break down in the non-dark humanoid, any contact with a humanoid under the dark reign would activate the infection in the predisposed genetics. This had to be solved since the non-dark stellar races were dependent on the trade from the systems under the dark ones and the non-dark stellar humanoids often had to visit or encounter races under the dark ones.

Five types of template and integrated genetics were then unfolded in the DE2 quadrant. The genetics lay the foundation of the racial organic form and its personality in the 4th to 6th dimensions, as well as its abilities to process light coding and by this generate consciousness. The combinations of genetics thus define the type of consciousness that is able to unfold from the vortexes of the DE2 energy system. The LPU level one energy system is similar to the DE2 energy system, since they are built on the same ancient technology.

1. The insectoid genetics cultivate the ability to work with the light coding of the quantum flux fields and the gridworks, i.e. all forms of construction work including holographic structures such as core crystals, buildings, cities and crafts to name a few.

2. The avian genetics foster the ability to do energy work such as handling the energies of a sub-field or timeline by inserting genetic resonance programs. The genetics give the ability to grow connections between genetics and the gridworks, the ability to create e.g. portals, timelines and so forth from the gridworks using the genetics etc, i.e. what we call magic.

3. The reptoid genetics give the ability to work with genetics, the energy system, the organic form and creation of lifeforms in a new gridwork. The reptoid genetics give the ability to work with sorts of advanced sciences and prefer the scientific angle in all consciousness abilities, hence when the reptoid genetics or TEGs are added, the personality becomes highly scientific. Naturally the reptoid genetics, because of its strength, are also used in warriors of all sorts, from priestly avian warriors to common reptilian strength and superhumans.

4. The mammal genetics give the ability to unfold capacities of political, societal, economic and similar community structures and are often found in the council members of the stellar communities, also within the DE2D4 and DE2D5 systems. Here the elders have got mammal TEGs added to do the diplomatic or political work as leaders and creators of societal structures.

5. The soul genetics hold the ability to self-heal and restore the LPU genetics, including the regressed, back to their original HM setting, if an individual hold these genetics. They are rare in the new stellar races though.

Understanding the TEGs

Technologically enhanced genetics:

- Generate consciousness from modified or fragmented soul genetics.
- Are either linked up to the gridworks in the non-crystalline areas or to soul matrices in the crystalline areas.
- Are able to project the consciousness of a lower dimensional energy system into a higher dimension.
- Can produce the idea of a higher self, because the projecting consciousness field is not directly linked to the personality.
- Are basically artificial intelligence and consciousness.
- Is the foundation in all hybridized and engineered biological lifeforms.
- They can be modified into becoming dark, submitting the consciousness traits of a dark one.

The first generation of TEGs are able to activate the self-healing abilities of the soul genetics and by this restore the genetics in the template and the level one energy system back into the original soul potentials that entered the LPU.

The second generation of TEGs does not have the same level of self-healing abilities, but they are useful in the restoration work of the soul genetics since they hold integrated information of how to work with the soul genetics, sorting out the merged-in TEGs from the integrated genetics.

The third and forth generations of TEGs hold no self-healing features and no information of how to work with the soul genetics.

Overview of the New Stellar Races

(Only a few is shown here since there are many thousand races)

Insectoid Races
- Mantids (Insectoid-reptoid TEGs)
- Tall Grays (Insectoid)
- Nature Spirits (Insectoid-avian TEGs)
- Dows (Insectoid-biological human)

Avian Races
- Arcturians (Avian)
- Dragon Moth (Avian-insectoid TEGs)
- LWB and RWBs (Avian-Mammal/Mammal TEGs)
- Thothians (Avian-Dark Mammal TEGs)

Reptoid Races
- Maldakian Settlers (Reptoid)
- Draco-reptilians and Draconians (Regressed reptoid)
- Lizards (Avian-Reptoid)
- Aryans (Reptoid-Mammal)
- Pleiadians (Mammal-Reptoids TEGs)

Mammal Races
- Sirian A (Mammal)
- Sirian B (Mammal-Reptoids)
- Maia-Pleiadians (Reptoid-Mammal)
- Winged Mammals (Mammal-Avian)
- No Name (Forms of Mammal-Insectoids)

Understanding the Creation of the LPRF Races

Question: What is a seed race?

Answer: A seed race is a specific term relating to a race or a group of entities joining into a specific reality field where they investigate and explore certain possibilities of that reality field. A seed race does as a rule not belong to that specific reality field but is "seeded" there, i.e. originate from other reality fields. A seed race also imply the making of a reality field by combining the khundarays of other reality fields and into that combined and created reality field. The partakers of the project step down and take on form according to the energetic set up of that reality field to be able to seed new races there.

Question: Working through a lifeform in a lower area?

Answer: It means connecting to a consciousness level telepathically advising, giving directions and serve as supervisors. Or by directly taking on a form within the race to become fully integrated into that reality field, albeit having the genetics and original form positioned on the original level of existence. Sometimes races from higher reality fields enjoyed stepping down to understand the perimeters of the lower LPRF or to invoke a new genetic combination within an existing race. This is called *vertical integration*.

Vertical merging is when a higher positioned entity projects his or her consciousness into the radiation field of a personality in a lower area. In this way the lower leveled humanoid gets instructions on how to perform certain things, needed to develop the reality field, i.e. council members and similar stakeholders of a reality field.

Question: Vertical and horizontal integration?
Answer: Conjunctions of light fields with a reality field can create a new form into which the makers project their consciousness.

Contrary to the seed races and the working through another form, appropriately called *vertical integration,* the creation of a new form on the same plane of existence is called *horizontal integration.*

Horizontal integration is performed by expanding the radiation, vibration and quantum fields from two entities into one combined field, from which a new light field emerges; the third light field or "the child" is the result. Creation of new lifeforms always demands a triangle of light coding and genetics to create new forms.

A vertical created race holds higher amounts of soul genetics and is therefore often responsible for seeding of new races "from above". A horizontal created race can hold soul genetics but mostly they function within their own types of LPRF genetics and are only seeding new specimens of the same LPRF genetics.

Infusion of genetics can also be done by horizontal and vertical merging.

Question: What is genetic identity?
Answer: Genetic identity holds the idea of similarity in genetics. It is a kind of sharing of genetics making the contributor and the receiver able to unfold the same type of consciousness. If a humanoid shared some of his or her genetics by expanding the three fields into another humanoid creating similar interference patterns, the two humanoids would exchange genetics, if the genetics hold the same basic genetic pattern. This is performed to restore genetics in the other humanoid.

A humanoid can also transfer some of his or her integrated genetics by dividing the genetics in the three vortexes and transfer the divided units into another humanoid, if this humanoid has been depleted of his or her genetics. This can unfortunately be done by force as well and the word extraction is appropriate here. Willingly shared genetics equals transfer. Unwillingly equals extraction.

The races in the lower LPRFs were created by:
- Vertical integration.
- Horizontal integration.
- Genetic identity to the ones that contributed. All the races in the lower LPRFs were under the protectorate of the higher leveled LPRF3-LPRF5 races, being genetically interlinked.

The LPRF3 and LPRF4 races had three types of consciousness:
- Pure genetic influx from the LPRF5s.
- Genetic merging from similar LPRF3 and LPRF4 races.
- Genetic transfer from other seeded LPRF3 and LPRF4 races.

The General Level

The goal of the general level is to give information upon the foundation of our universe among other things. History alone is not enough, the settings are important too.

On Dimensions, Densities and Timelines

The HM Holographic Resonance Fields

The holographic resonance fields (the HRFs) consist of light coding from the previous evolutionary cycle. They hold variations of the light coding from the sub-levels of the previous cycles and consequently have dissimilar combinations of light coding. Some HRFs actually hold light coding from other even more ancient cycles within the fields of light coding of the previous cycle. These HRFs are rare and they are only connected to the highest evolved soul races being able to control and transform these ancient and very difficult energies. Soul races are set into HRFs matching their evolutionary step and capacity, i.e. only the ones able to transform the light coding, will attend the challenges of each of the HRFs.

Soul races shift between the HRFs as they develop and transform their genetics through the interaction with light coding. This is called progression of the genetics. Progression happens by living in the HRFs on an individual basis. This means that an individual true human can elevate by will and fast progression. Others just follow the minor cycles of progression, which are called elevation cycles. The elevation cycles control the collective shift of the soul group genetics from one level of the HRF to another and they are part of the overall and major evolutionary cycles.

The LPU Energy Gridworks

Energy or light coding generates two kinds of holographic grids: 1) the grid inside an energy system in LPU humanoids and 2) the gridworks of a reality field. The gridworks stem from the khundarays and are linked up to the central sun of the LPU. There are no gridworks in the HM. Aside from the khundarays extended from the core, producing the foundation for everything in the LPU including the humanoid form and energy system, the gridworks generate reality fields, when activated.

New gridworks are activated by the genetics in an energy system connecting to the gridwork, e.g. if an energy system is entering a new level of the LPU due to alterations in genetics, making it impossible for the genetics to stay in the present gridwork. When this happens the genetics are shifted to new gridworks activating the gridworks. The gridworks are able to unfold an energy system directly from the gridwork. This happens when new races are seeded into a gridwork by the will of higher LPU races, called vertical integration. However horizontal integration is also possible from one gridwork to another, where the same type of genetics is expanded and by this activates new gridworks.

The LPU Reality Fields and Timelines
The interaction of energy systems, genetics and gridworks create a reality field. The genetics link up to the khundarays in the gridwork and from here the foundation of a reality field is generated, where the energy system can unfold its presence or existence. Thus a reality field only needs one energy system with genetics to unfold.

The difference between a gridwork and reality fields amount to the timelines, which are the result of a reality field as it is perceived, wanted and unfolded through the active use of the light coding of the gridworks through the energy systems linked up to the gridworks. *Gridworks* are thus the energizers of the energy systems, whereas *reality fields* are the surrounding results of the gridwork light coding, processed through the genetics of the energy system. *Timelines* are made by the genetic activity (conscious processing of light coding in the gridworks) of the inhabitants in a reality field. Timelines and reality fields are interconnected and can be difficult to discern from each other, since they both generate the surroundings.

There can be several timelines in a reality field, generating sub-fields of the main reality field. Thus one reality field holds divisions of what is manifested due to the timelines. The reality field is generated by the central quote of genetics inserted into the gridworks, and the timelines are the sub-field generated by the small variations of the genetics and hence the conscious processing of light coding from the lower template, and through this the gridworks.

Timelines are both individual and collective. Individual timelines create variations in perception of the main reality field because of dissimilarities in genetics, whereas collective timelines are unfolding the reality perceived by the majority. If the collective timelines are altered, the main reality field changes as well.

Thus reality fields can be controlled by higher dimensional races affecting the genetics of the majority living in that reality field, or the influencing races can generate a tidal wave of changes by affecting many individual sets of genetics and hence the individual timelines, and over time making these join into one large timeline, changing the main field. Telepathic contact through individual genetics is used in the latter case of changes.

The Densities and Dimensions

Densities (DE) arose from the timeline event, where the explosion of the mixed core of the Sirius star cluster and the infected gridworks transformed the reality fields of the LPRF3 and LPRF2 systems into densities instead. Densities are thus used as the terminology of the post-timeline event reality fields, but are in fact the same as reality fields. The densities are divided into three sub-density fields, called dimensions. *Dimensions* arise from the merged-in TEGs of the energy systems and the affected gridworks cf. the interconnection between gridworks and genetics, in contrast to the LPU reality fields connected to the central sun. However the later generations of the TEGs have been engineered to be able to connect to the non-infected gridworks. For the sake of simplicity I have kept the name of the lower template as the gridwork template of the post-timeline event lower template instead of calling it a dimensional template. Most of the ones who get a template reading are from the ancient stellar races, where the gridworks were under the transformation into dimensions. Hence gridworks resemble the dimensions of the densities.

Densities = Reality Fields of the DE3 and DE2
Dimensions = Gridworks of the DE3 and DE2

The LPU holds reality fields with sub-fields, called areas and densities with sub-fields called dimensions. A universe is composed of all of the densities and can be viewed as a pyramid, where the top is the core. From the core the reality fields and densities unfold.

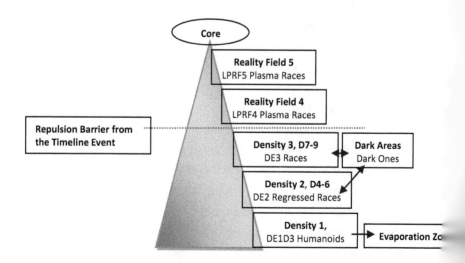

LPU Dimensional Bridges

The LPU dimensional bridges are intersection points of dimensions and densities, i.e. where dimensions and densities cross or intersect each other. The intersection points of a density and its gridworks (dimensions) can be seen as the position, where one dimension or a whole density shifts into a new one.

Each intersection point therefore generates *a dimensional bridge* (a star gate) due to the differences in dimensions and the densities they stem from. Because of the dissimilarities in dimensions and in the features of the densities, the dimensional bridges differ from each other. Hence the dimensional bridges do not have the same facilities of enabling:

1. **Entry** (only able to enter a dimension).
2. **Exit** (only able to leave a dimension).
3. **Exit & entry** (able to enter and leave a dimension).
4. **Connection** (the bridges are used as communication devises through the genetics – this differs from telepathy, where the genetics can connect to each other due to their similarities. Telepathy is done by projection of consciousness into the radiation field of the one holding the identical genetics, be it copies or from the same racial generation of genetics.
5. **Transformation** (is only achievable when the energy system has developed the genetics and is done with the dimension and thus elevates, or has integrated TEGs enabling the same thing to take place).
6. **Dimensional shift** (can only be done by insertion of advanced TEGs enabling this, or by manipulation of the energy system,

done by the individual having full control over the energy system, the integrated genetics and the upper template and from here shift their organic form from one level to another.

The use of the dimensional bridge is determined by the integrated genetics of the level one energy system. The integrated genetics are for their part determined by the possibilities of the template genetics and these can be soul genetics or TEGs, or both.

Many TEGs are engineered specifically to enable the humanoid form to utilize the dimensional bridges in one of the six variations. Other TEGs are engineered to enable the energy system to access the dimensional bridges, leaving the organic form temporarily behind in a hibernated state in the dimension that is left behind. Then the traveling level one energy system, with the personality intact in spite of the hibernated organic form, can take on another dimensional form in the visiting dimension by inserting TEGs to enable the energy system to match the new dimensional light coding.

Engineered TEGs have many functions and the most important is the dimensional bridges, especially seen in the light of the fact that most of the regressed races as well as the new stellar races are not able to utilize the dimensional bridges.

Most of the dimensional bridges were generated shortly after the timeline event by the ancient stellar races and thus link up to older generations of TEGs and genetics. Given that the later stellar races have little resemblance to their ancient forefathers, the genetics in the DE1D3 humanoids have a big role to play in why we have been sealed off and utilized as we have. The sealing off of the personality in the level one energy system, have enabled the later stellar races to utilize the dimensional bridges by temporarily borrowing (or buying) a sealed off energy system. It has also been done by harvesting the template genetics and inserting these into their energy systems (most of the foreign genetics are repulsed, but they can work fine enough for a short period granting the dimensional access) and by extracting the integrated viable genetics from sealed off energy systems, leaving the emptied level one energy system to decay in the reintegration cycles and so forth. The extracted genetics are utilized as the core in a TEG, enabling the TEG to perform the same features that are in the extracted genetics. Thus the harvesting and extracting of genetics have to be seen in the light of the dimensional bridges too and not only as food for the dark ones. The dimensional bridges with the facilities of entry and exit are mostly utilized by organic forms, i.e. the later stellar races travelling from one dimension to another.

Bridges, where it is possible to transform energetically (shifting in and out of organic forms) are utilized by humanoids having shed off their organic form and now are positioned in the energy system with its template getting ready to take on a new organic form in another dimension, either higher or lower all depending on the quanta of the genetics. Humanoids with templates holding a higher ratio of TEGs do not need to progress their genetics into higher levels of quanta in the vibration field since they are fueled by the artificial genetics often set up to be able to unfold organic forms in a range of dimensions.

The connection facility is part of the dimensional bridges between races unfolding in the same dimension. The stellar races can connect energetically through the connecting dimensional bridge with the purpose of sharing information, goods and similar items.

The Dimensional Bridges of DE1D3
The dimensional bridges of our reality field are special compared to the bridges of the other dimensions. This has to do with the blueprint in the gridworks, as well as the infused soul genetics of the HMDE3s, enabling the gridworks of the DE1D3 to house and fuel the genetics of *all races* in the LPU and outside in the HM. Furthermore the quantum

flux fields, the DE1D3 consisted of before the DE1D3 colonies came to be, morphed in and out of manifestation (probabilities) generating oscillation. The oscillation of the DE1D3 quantum flux fields made the holographic fields unstable – one moment the probabilities were manifested, the next they were not - and dimensional bridges were then impossible to stabilize since the merging points between the DE1D3 and the other dimensions morphed in and out of existence. The HMDE3s and the ancient stellar races from the DE1D3 colonies solved this, back then, by stabilizing the quantum flux fields through the insertion of 12 crystal pillars.[129]

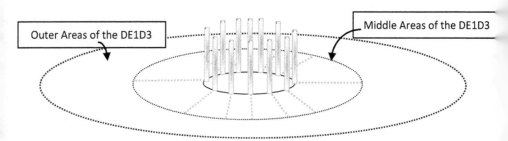

Above is a 2D illustration of the core DE1D3 areas with the 12 pillars. The middle areas generate the blueprint of the middle DE1D3, which naturally changed with the additional blueprint of the enclosure giving the reality field its oval form (added with the residual energies from the astral plane giving us the type of reality we have today) and the outer areas are shown as the rest of the DE1D3s linking up to the

---

[129] The crystal pillars are generated from holographic light coding with the same geometrical structure and thus not able to change according to genetics or any other type of interaction, giving them the features of crystals as we understand it. The grid of the pillars is fixed in the 3rd dimension and link directly up to the core of the planet. Since the core consist of gridworks from Maldak and the former Er′Th, the 12 crystal pillars are fueled by these gridworks and thus link back up to the past and the present. The core gridwork of our reality field hold all the abilities of all of the races that have unfolded from the beginning of the LPU up until now.

4-6th dimension via the dimensional bridges. The access from the 3rd dimension and to the 4th, 5th and 6th dimension amount to 18 bridges (3+4+5+6), however there is actually 21, because three hidden 3rd dimensional bridges are positioned in the Pacific Ocean, where the Hyperborean Isle will resurface; all in all the dimensional bridges amount to 21 in total. The 21 dimensional bridges represent the 21 humanoid races the DE1D3 is able to house or fuel genetically via the gridworks and the blueprints imbedded in them (the inner three races being the true DE1D3 earth humanoids that retracted to Hallow Earth and by this sealing off the three inner bridges, which link to Hallow Earth).

Together the pillars and the bridges keep the whole DE1D3 system stable. The bridges are an important part of the future scenarios given that the areas holding functional bridges can contact the other dimensions and thus are in power of all the knowledge they need to control the planet. The active dimensional bridges also prevent the areas surrounding the bridges from becoming unstable, if and when a pole shift happens.

The areas with nonfunctional bridges are to face a rough time in the future because the dimensional bridges are the last thing keeping the quantum flux field stable when the crystal pillars cannot hold the quantum flux field steady anymore. The pillars are under the process of dissolving, due to the link up to the astral barrier and astral plane, and the high level of decaying these energies are in. The light coding of the pillars are deteriorating as we speak.

As the grid of the pillars dissolve the remaining coding will retract to Hallow Earth because of light coding similarity (the containing grid is gone) and the quantum flux fields of the DE1D3 will return to their original unsettled state. In this case only the dimensional bridges will keep the countries and landmasses, as we know them. All other areas will return to the morphing in and out, unless they are inhabited by citizens with a strong genetic set up being able to counteract the instability in the flux fields.

Overview of the Dimensional Bridges

D3	Easter Island	**Destroyed**	*Exit/Dimensional Shift*
	Pacific Ocean	**Active**	*All Facilities/Secret*
	India	**Sealed off**	*Connection/Transformation*
	Japan	**Active**	*Entry/Exit*

D4	Iraq/Sumer	**Sealed off**	*Entry/Connection*
	Israel	**Active**	*Exit/Entry*
	England	**Active**	*Connection*
	Peru	**Destroyed**	*Exit/Entry/Transformation*

D5	France	**Active**	*Connection*
	South Pole	**Active**	*Entry/Transformation*
	Russia	**Active**	*Exit/Entry*
	China	**Active**	*Entry/Connection*
	Egypt (Sphinx)	**Sealed off**	*Exit/Entry/Connection/ Transformation*

D6	Crete	**Destroyed**	*Exit/Entry/Connection*
	South Africa	**Destroyed**	*Exit/Entry/Transformation*
	North Pole	**Active**	*Exit/Dimensional Shift*
	Australia	**Active**	*Exit/Entry/Connection*
	Tibet	**Sealed off**	*Exit/Entry/Connection*
	Brazil	**Active**	*Exit/Entry*

The active 3D dimensional bridge in Japan is under the control of the Japanese LWBs, holding a mix of ancient DE1D3 humanoid genetics (from the ones that were slaughtered) and avian genetics. The bridge in Japan is one of the oldest. The three bridges in the Pacific Ocean are part of the Hyperborean Isle and will be used in the rising of the landmass.

The active 4D dimensional bridges are under the control of the LWBs and the OWO (to some extent the RWBs can utilize them as well but only through negotiations or trade of knowledge).

All active 5D bridges are controlled by the reptilian-reptoid races (the reptilians hold regressed genetics with the reptilian features, whereas the reptoids have the ancient human-like features) present in the DE1D3.

The dimensional bridge in 6D Brazil is controlled by the Sirian Bs. The bridge in Tibet is controlled by the Sirian A descendants through in the lineage of the Lamas; when the last superior lama is gone, the bridge will be taken over by the Chinese and sealed off since they do not hold viable Sirian A genetics. However genetic experiments are going on from various factions to copy the ancient Sirian A genetics to gain control over this bridge.

The bridge in Australia is under the control of the Maia-Pleiadians. The last active bridge in the North Pole is connected to Hallow Earth and is under their control.

Bridge Zones and the Holographic Teachings

One goal of our energy work could be to be able to travel through the dimensional bridges of the DE2 system back into the timelines of the Sirius A system, being connected to the HM. To do this we need to activate our ancient genetics, mostly the first and second generation of TEGs or true human genetics. The true human genetics are the same as soul genetics. If we hold the level of mammal genetics, these have to be developed into the level, where they are able to bridge to the Sirian A areas. The dimensional bridges are still there. Another goal could be to gain access to the holographic teachings to be able to enter the bridge zones back to the HM. So what are the bridge zones and the holographic teachings?

The Bridge Zones

The bridge zones are the bridges connecting the HM and the LPU. The bridge zones are not placed in time and space as in a location, but are interdimensional. The bridge zones are activated by the soul genetics, which are unfolded into the energy system of a specific dimension. The soul genetics thus have to be activated on the dimensional level, i.e. be integrated into the level one energy system and utilized on that dimension, to be able to activate and connect to the bridge zones. Hence many of the first three generations of energy systems[130] hold an inserted distortion field making the soul genetics unable to reconnect to the bridge zones.

---

[130] The new stellar races cannot connect to the bridge zones even if they wanted, unless they hold a high quote of soul genetics, which is unusual. If and when a time comes where they get the knowledge of the HM and if the new stellar races want to return to the HM, a lot of work has to be done with their TEGs and energy systems.

Besides, only when the soul genetics have regained the original soul potentials are we able to travel through the bridge zones, in our level one energy system.

The original soul potentials equal the soul genetics we entered with, or at least hold the same vibration and radiation levels.[131] The original soul potentials are obtained the moment the template is emptied of soul genetics and all genetics are integrated into the level one energy system, i.e. in any dimension where this becomes possible and by this is able to transform the organic body in full to be able to shed off all less-progressive energies and undo the modifications, which were done to the soul genetics to enable them to function inside the LPU.

When the soul genetics are fully integrated into the energy system and have regained the original soul potentials, they are able to pass the bridge zones just by wanting it. For most in living in the density areas this happens after the shedding off of the organic form, where they stand in the level one energy system. However how to do this and how to enter the bridging zones is *not something we can get as instructions from outer sources or teachers*. It has to be re-learned from within, which for most humanoids, having depleted the soul genetics to lesser or higher extent, is somewhat difficult, hence it is complicated to regain the original soul potential.

The Holographic Teachings

All bridge zones have a set of holographic information linked to them and a humanoid, when it has activated enough of its soul genetics into the level one energy system, can connect on an inner level to the holographic teachings via the activated and integrated soul genetics. Through the activated soul genetics in the level one energy system,

---

[131] The understanding of the vibration and radiation level is part of the second year.

the personality of the level one energy system is able to receive the instructions on how to regain the full potentials of the soul genetics to enable the soul genetics to return to the HM, as they were when they entered the LPU.

Unfortunately the holographic teachings have been tampered with in most dimensions making it tricky for the stellar humanoid to obtain the correct information. The bridge zone teachings of the 4th and 5th dimension have been distorted with forged instructions, leading the stellar humanoid back to the LPU. Many of the bridge zones have been shut down by messing with their light coding, in which case the genetics cannot attach and unfold the instructions. When a bridge zone is tampered with, the teachings are still intact but useless, given that the teachings and the bridge zone are interconnected. The next generation of earth-stellar humanoids will solve this.

Because of the tampering of the bridge zones, only from the 6th dimension and up are the zones and their teachings intact. The 3rd dimensional bridge zone and teachings are intact as well, but this is placed in the DE1D3 areas outside the astral barrier connected to the hyperborean reality fields. These can only be accessed by the next phase of the earth-stellar humanoids that arise with the Hyperborean Isle. The bridge zones to the HM in the 6th dimension were left under the control of the Pleiadian-Sirian A and thus the teachings of the 4th and 5th dimension have been placed here as well as a short sum up to make the 6th dimensional teachings understandable.

The 7th dimensional recordings are highly technical and difficult to grasp, which is why most of the stellar humanoids that manage to reset their genetics aim for the 6th dimensional bridge zones.

The holographic teachings are interactive holograms, flashing back to the viewer the levels of information needed to enter the bridge zone. The teachings instruct the stellar humanoid in how to reverse the LPU light coding of the energy system and template, which is slightly reversed compared to the HM but not as reversed as the reversed light coding of the astral barrier. The undoing of the LPU reversed light coding and the full integration of the template genetics into the level one energy system enables the stellar humanoid to transform and shift out of that specific dimension and into the HM.

The OWOs altered the light coding of the 3rd and 4th dimensional bridge zones, sealing off the teachings. Later on the draco-reptilians added distortions to the 5th dimensional bridge zones. From that point on no one could get access to the bridge zones in the 3rd, 4th and 5th dimension or get access to the teachings. The teachings of how to get to the HM were hidden and later on forgotten.

The First Access to the Recordings
The teaching from the holographic interactive teacher is reflecting back the needed level to work with as the first thing.
Here is an example:

It is an imperative that you learn to work consciously and correctly with the genetics. Otherwise you will be stumped in your attempts to progress in the last phase of the journey towards the full freedom of consciousness. Since our possibilities of intervention are limited due to the laws of individual return by effort and means performed by the individual stellar being, we cannot intervene "and make things right"; only you can do this by working correctly with your possibilities in your energy systems. Nevertheless we can give you the tools and instruments to do the needed work.

The 4th Dimensional Recordings
Then the teachings go into a more general level, when the individual level is understood:

You have now accessed the 4th dimensional holographic teachings. This level is made to show you the basic steps of the freedom process

211

you voluntarily have agreed to take upon yourself. At some level, you have discovered the regressed reality field, you presently are a part of or you have by your own means crossed into the bridge zone and are now part of the returning programs. No matter what the origin of the access is, the information you need is to be given according to your genetics and the level of progression they hold.

Unfortunately we cannot show you all of the details you need to work with since this recording was made in the very early stages and as the future has shown us, the evolution within the less-progressive universe, related to the densities, will evolve to such a degree that we do not hold the correct technological or means of consciousness to cover all grounds. However we trust you to have found a way to this level of information otherwise you would not be able to interact with the teachings.

As you know the first steps to enter the bridge zone is to let go of all you perceive yourself to be. The determination of the sense of self is built upon influenced genetics of which you are an expression. You embody combinations of genetics changed into different senses of self and selfhood.

The sense of selfhood and separation is one of the most important illusions to keep up the areas you presently are part of, no matter what you call it, i.e. depending on what timeframe you read this recording from.

This sense of selfhood and the ability to rule by the means and ideas of this self, uphold the engineered energy systems. The sense of selfhood creates an illusion of being an individual, holding fantastic and unique possibilities better than others unfolding the same organic structure. The truth is that there is no sense of self or selfhood. There is a constructed reality holding holographic light coding, unfolding the holographic fields the energy systems interact with. When the sense of selfhood vanishes, the perception of separation between the energy system, its personality and the surrounding reality field disappears. The genetic coding of the energy systems is upheld by the interacting light coding fields.

The light coding will be visible to the ones being able to look for the mathematical matrices (the grids of light coding) controlled and directed by the light coding found in dimensional surroundings.

The lack of progression is not to be found in the surrounding fields, but in the changed genetics inserted into the energy systems. The genetics are the source of the interacting light coding that unfolds the sense of self with its projected images of restriction. Therefore the energy systems with the inserted genetics are a combined program. The restriction is not to be found in the surroundings but in its source: the energy systems into which the genetics have been inserted. Thus the way to freedom lies within the means of expression and existence, which is contained in the changed genetics. Therefore the changed genetics are both the source of self and existence, and thus the restriction, but also the means that lead to the way of freedom.

From the Blog

Get the future insights on the blog. I have added some of the posts here to show how quickly things change.

Incoming Races from the Future around year 2800

"In the year 2017, 2047 in our time, an unknown galactic race enters the solar system. They will become the game changer of your system. Up until now the Sirian Bs (the CSBs) have had the upper hand solving the infection problem with their crystalline technologies and getting rid of the infection that turns the merged-in genetics into dark substance as well as preventing the TEGs from breaking down. The crystalline technology with its 6-12 stranded template (all TEGs) and silicate body are implementing faster this time (our presence speed things up) and most of your race accepts the offer and joins the Sirian B collective of freed stellar races. The incoming galactic races stem from a foreign quadrant of the LPU, our present cycle of evolution, and have one main goal to achieve. To complicate things they are from the future that follows after the Sirian Bs take over all of the DE2 areas with their crystalline agenda. In the future the crystalline races turn into a species that will become a threat to all other races of the LPU. As the eternal and frozen in consciousness in the silicate matrix body stays in its outer steady state, the encapsulated infected TEGs and isolated TEGs with the potentiality to break down undergo an internal transmutation process where the crystalline energy body and organic form is altered from within into a new race which has been termed the "Ones holding no living soul."

Around year 2800 your time this race becomes a huge problem for rest of the stellar races in the future LPU following the dimensionality of these races. The infection that the crystalline DE2 thought they had beaten, arises to new levels built upon the crystalline technologies and instead of infecting the living genetics, it now only eats from the crystalline structures. The infection in the future does not only feed of the genetics as hitherto but now it begins feeding of the LPU itself. Huge chunks of the LPU will in the future freeze into dark crystalline reality fields where nothing or nobody can escape.

To prevent this future, the future galactic races of our present timeframe, the year 2800 your time, have gathered together a group of volunteers to take the journey back to your timeline and present timeframe to prevent this. They will arrive in year 2017 your time-frame (DE1 time) and 2047 our timeframe (DE3 time). Since we are already present in the future they have landed here and are now in negotiations with us to solve the problem. Due to the time delay in DE1 we can only pass this information on and leave it up to you to take action.

Now what is the objective of these unknown future races? First and foremost they are a symbol of change and development. They hold a higher degree of older versions of LPU genetics and very little TEGs. As the DE2 crystallizes and more races change into the silicate matrix body, more of the stellar races around the DE2 become aware of the danger that the crystalline areas begin to pose to the natural evolution of the LPU. So they observe the crystalline races and learn from this and as a result isolate themselves from the crystalline areas. New DE2 races arise with the help from the DE3 areas and all issues with the TEGs and merged-in genetics are solved in full.

After a couple of 100 years in peace within the other DE2 and DE3 stellar races, the problem of the dark crystalline races arises. In the beginning the future races, now following the original evolutionary plans for our present cycle and its holographic (light coding based) universe, are not concerned but after the spreading into certain areas of the future non-regressed and non-crystalline areas, actions have to be taken. And thus this delegation. The concern is this: Since the faraway future stellar races know how dangerous the crystalline matrix body becomes for all of us in this cycle, these future races hold no mercy. Their objective is to get rid of all technology that leads to the crystalline future. And in this all templates and energy bodies that in your time is undergoing the crystallization process.

What does this mean? It literally means that all holding TEGs will get these eradicated after year 2017, when they arrive and with them powerful technology to secure this. For most of the DE2s or DE1s holding this technology it will mean loss of dimensional awareness and a setback to their natural level of progression.

The future races prefer underdeveloped species developing LPU genetics naturally instead of the ones running on TEGs. This will in turn alter their future profoundly into a less advanced future. However all stellar races collaborating on this have agreed on it and are prepared for the setback. Measures are being taken as we speak to prepare for the major shift in holographic settings as well as level of progression of the non-regressed and non-crystalline races. Our councils are debating this now, i.e. the effects of this in our reality field and the future we presently are in. We traveled back to prevent the takeover by the pro-crystalline races, but nothing further. For us this was a thing that could be solved in the future, that is following the DE3 future, as in the rest of the LPU. However this changes everything as well as the work you need to do in your timeframe and what it will lead to in our reality as well as within the future races of year 2800 (DE4 areas).

Races holding viable genetics will be visited and assisted in how to progress in a faster pace to circumvent the loss of a whole sector (the present DE2) into a more primitive state. Without the TEGs the present organic form will break down and the DE2 races will be set back to the original level they had after the Reptilian Riots. This means large civilizations will return to the state of mind and organic forms of the older cycle and thus a huge loss of consciousness.

The future plans we had made with the ones inside your reality field choosing the non-regressed and non-crystalline path will change to fit the new obstacles. You will be assisted to a higher degree than hitherto and the genetic progression technologies that are unfolded in the future races will be shared with us in our present timeframes, first in our reality field and then in yours after 2017. From being a minority you will after 2017 become the ones "in the know" and thus in charge of the needed work that has to be done.

Is it in order to intervene in this way in a whole sector? As far as we are concerned yes, if it secures the future of us all. To us evolving in the lower densities, the intervention card has not been one we were able to pull unless original genetic infused humans voluntarily agreed to shift from the regressed consciousness and back into the original LPU settings. As long as the DE2 races prefer their regressed and crystalline version of the level one energy system and template, then we have had no say in this. LPRF3 genetically infused races cannot beat the artificial crystalline technology, since the crystalline technology transforms all versions of LPU genetics into artificial TEGs. To us it has been the road of no return and thus we have built around the DE2s instead of interfering with them. We have only worked with the ones remembering their origin. This is about to change. Let's put it this way: the battle we thought we were to take in another timeframe has now been dragged into our present level of existence and this will become a game changer for us all.

Our goal of sharing this is to give you the information, so you can choose wisely. If you prefer the TEG technology, you should be aware that this will not give you more than a couple of 100 years before you becomes a threat to everything and anyone around you. Our hope is that you will join the soul infused evolution instead and not take on the offerings from the DE2s that are getting stronger every day in your reality field, selling you the idea of a long lost 12 stranded template that is your birthright. You are not regaining something you have lost; you are altering into an agenda instigated to win you over, simply because the CSBs belive that they have found the solution to everything "evil". Little do they know that they themselves will become the biggest threat of all evil we have ever encountered in this cycle.

Choose wisely even though it might mean that you will be set back in your LPU evolution. If you do not do this on your own, others will do it for you, so why shift into something that will be taken away from you again? It is better to stay with the LPU genetics you have and then collaborate with the soul progression technologies that are coming your way in a couple of years, if all goes well."

Now I have got this message from my DE3 group, and thus it is not manipulation. However they are barely beginning their work with the DE4 soul races and thus we as always have to be cautious. For me this is just another reason not to choose the DE2 teachings that flourishes on the Internet and all over the place. As I look into the DE4 races from the year 2800 they seem threatening to me simply because they are more powerful than me and my animal form reacts with fear to this, as it should. But being more powerful does not mean being evil; just something I have to get used to be in contact with.

A Vision

In very ancient times there were no animals in this system. There were only stellar humanoids, which as you know are upright entities having two arms, legs, a torso and a head. However many of the stellar humanoid races have animal features today, as in having a lion's head, perhaps a tale etc. The depictions of the Egyptian gods as well as the Hindu and Mesopotamian gods depict this very clearly.

In the vision I saw how the stellar humanoids were captured and altered genetically, returning them into the square form (being on all four legs again) by manipulating their DE2 holographic energy system. They were turned into a previous evolutionary state by purpose of the other regressed races that arose after the timeline event. These manipulated stellar humanoids, which did not have the regressive gene pool were captured and altered with the purpose of being sent to our planet.

The suddenly there came to be animals on this planet.

Later on when other regressed stellar humanoids entered this planet and they saw the animal life forms and thought it was a beautiful planet, they started to eat the meat to survive. It was totally unknown to them that they were actually eating their stellar brothers and sisters, now having lost their telepathic abilities and thus could not communicate with the incoming stellar humanoids to tell them that they were trapped inside of the old version of the humanoid form, but that they were still conscious beings, just like them.

This atrocity made the incoming stellar humanoids bound to the planet and they could not leave it again as a result of the horrifying thing they had done.

The Sirian B-Reptoid Wars

Apparently from one of the timelines in our reality field, the hunt for the reptilians (regressed reptoid genetics) begins and it begins on our planet. This hunt is instigated by some ideologies of the Sirian Bs (extreme crystalline faction) and will lead to a huge galactic war in the near-future between the Sirian Bs and the reptilian-reptoid races.

Most of the reptilian-reptoid races are hunted down during and after this war, both benevolent and less-benevolent and the effects of this echo out into the rest of our galaxy affecting all lifeforms here. The implications of the hunting down is that ALL humanoids having reptilian-reptoid genetics (all races inclusive) are hunted down and slaughtered or undergo a voluntarily separation of reptoid genetics from their template and energy system.

In the end the Sirian Bs having a high level of reptoid genetics themselves, get wiped out as well. The Sirian Bs begin the war to eradicate the reptilian genetics in other stellar races and end up disappearing due to a lack of genetic resemblance to their own reality field.

In this future, there are very little humanoids or any living stellar races left, given that mostly all of the races of today and the near future hold reptilian or reptoid genetics in some form. Thus the work implicates us all, on that timeline, which if we are not careful with the Sirian Bs, could become the collective timeline.

I have no problem with accepting this as a fact. First and foremost timelines are individual and collective and only the collective adjust the main reality field into new scenarios. The individual timelines only color the perception of the stellar humanoid. I have for a long time wondered, and mentioned in small portions, about the man-hunt that is going on with the reptilians here. There are factions out there blaming all on the reptilians as in them being the bad guys for all that is taking place; there are bad reptilians and some of them are working with the dark ones, but the real bad guys are the mammal-reptoid dark ones and the avian left wing brotherhoods; they are the ones in control of the part of the DE1D3 reality field, we call the planet.

We have to discern between the regressed reptilians and the reptoid humanoids: the reptilians hold reptoid regressed genetics and thus have the reptilian features, whereas the reptoids have human-like features.

See more on the videos part 1 and 2 on the Sirian B-Reptoid Wars.

Information from the Councils

In the whole of the less-progressive universe (the LPU) every density is based upon quantum flux fields (QFFs), where all energies act like we see it on the quantum level in our reality field. The only reason why our atoms are stable is because of the technology of the 12 crystal pillars preventing the holographic bits of our reality field from morphing in and out of existence. The DE1D3 reality field (our solar system) is hit harder by unstable QFFs due to the timeline event; mostly because of its artificial structure to begin with built by the LPRF3s.

All central positioned stars are what we call a sun if the star is positioned in the core of a reality field and by this provides the dimensional fields with photonic energies (light). Photonic energies are holographic coding extending from the khundarays attached to the central sun, or the artificial core of the LPU (Source). Khundarays enable a gridwork to unfold into an inhabitable area of the LPU, and by this generate a reality field or as it has been called after the timeline event, a density.

All stars are interlinked and are part of the khundaray network, enabling the stars to fuel the gridworks with sustaining energies, i.e. with both vibration and radiation energies. A star becomes a sun if it is the central star connecting several khundarays attached to other gridworks, but only if it interlinks to more than one gridwork and by this is interlinked to the other suns of that major field zone. A major field zone is what we call a system and it holds many suns. A system covers several sub-dimensions in one density and holds many different lifeforms and universes. All suns in a system have a sort of procession that from our perspective is undetectable since the procession takes million of years and humanity has not been around to observe the processions of the major field zones and their suns.

This means that a sun, with all of its gridworks, i.e. dimensions, will shift position over millions of years in our perspective of things. Naturally this is not due to "time" since time is an effect of the stable environment we live in and not a natural thing in the LPU.

Such a procession of a sun, interlinked to a density two (DE2) dimension 4 (DE2D4) minor universe in the outskirts of our system, is in these days (August 2015) entering our DE1D3 reality field in the 4th dimension. The entering of the DE2D4 sun and its gridworks are affecting the quantum flux fields in all three areas of our reality field and this leads to new political decisions. The entering of suns and their progression fields is a normal thing, so it is not a catastrophe but it poses an opportunity, which we cannot go undetected.

4D Quantum Sun entering our DE1D3
Reality Field

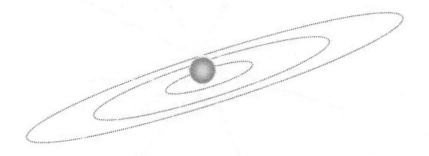

The entering sun is sustaining a very old universe, which has been left to its own after the regression took place in many of the DE2D5 and DE2D4 areas. This universe with its many minor inhabitable zones underwent a series of regressions altering all of the DE2D4 races present there, back into their animal state and from here the rest of the avian races left. The communities are now desolated and most of the animal lifeforms have died out due to lack of genetic infusion. The communities underwent the process of being civilized areas into a wilderness and from that level on the planets and their communities have been left to their own demise and processes. The regression has now stopped in this universe since there are no genetics attached to the gridworks to regress and by this the gridworks have reset to their pre-regressive state.

Thus the gridworks hold a major opportunity since they stem from some of the older khundaray systems. This means that the gridworks are able to process older versions of TEGs and genetics, which for a long time only the DE1D3 was able to. The DE1D3 holds, in its gridworks, the ability to work with all of the races of the LPU, covering all dimensions and densities which make the DE1D3 pretty special. But the entering sun poses an opportunity to the DE2D4 races present in our reality field, to take off and link the sun to their major field zone (the DE2D4 areas) and by this get the needed infusion of an old gridwork they need to severely. If they do this, they do not need the DE1D3 anymore which is a good thing. Naturally our goal is to return the DE1D3 to the correct owners (the true DE1D3 earth humanoids) and not letting it be exploited by the new stellar races, of which the DE2D4s are part. All of this is part of ongoing negotiations.

If the DE2D4 non-crystalline stellar races, linked to the outer DE1D3 areas, take this opportunity several scenarios are possible in the DE1D3 reality field, but before we go there it should be duly noted that it is a joyous opportunity for the avian races to regain the possibility to re-activate the ancient levels of their genetic lineages, because although the avian races have died out in that universe, the gridworks still hold the old avian racial blueprint and with this the possibility to re-engineer the original avian genetics from before the regression.

However two major influencing factors have to be taken into consideration, seen from our perspective, because even though we gladly let these races go, because the goal of the LPU is to undo the damages after the regression and the many clinical programs having been performed to circumvent the regression, and by this having damaged the racial gene pool in the LPU, it is not unproblematic to us if they pull out, because: the take over from the crystalline Sirian Bs and their allies (the CSBs), would get a stronger chance if the DE2D4 non-crystalline races leave, leaving only the avian races supporting the CBSs in the 4D. That is naturally not a good thing, since then the DE2D5 reptoid races would be the only races left to counteract the CSBs. And this would lead to either:

A) The future scenario where the CSBs change the DE2 and DE3 into crystalline densities, meddling with the gridworks by unfolding their steady state technologies and by this freeze the khundarays. Their goal is to detach themselves from the central sun (the artificial core called "Source") and the crystalline universes will eventually splinter, due to lack of khundarays infusions and by this generate a new type of crystal darkness, which the future benevolent races of the other universes linked up to the LPU cannot undo.

In this future the splintered crystalline areas will devour huge areas of all of the universes surrounding the LPU in an attempt to reset – a natural mechanism – but due to the crystalline state the gridworks cannot attach correctly to the khundarays of the other areas and instead they devour them. This darkness unfolds a whole new race (the splintered off crystalline races) and factions from these races have returned from the future to secure the detachment from the artificial central sun (they have many names on the internet, but I will not add more energy by using these names since the perception of them are full of astral energies, fear etc and by this I would add to the problem below). The CSBs see no connection to these races, since they cannot see the future effects of their endeavors with the crystalline technologies. They have lost the connection to the rest of the LPU by their separation from the central sun and their creation of the soul matrices, which they for now see as a good thing. For them the crystalline technologies give them full freedom to create new universes holding new types of dimensions in the former LPRF3 dark areas utilizing their soul matrix and strand technologies to seed humanoids there. They strongly believe they are doing a good thing.

The future splintered off crystalline races are already meddling with humanity being attached to the enclosure to secure that their future will unfold and they are influencing CSB stakeholders to make this happen.

They are also influencing certain factions of the LWBs supporting the CSBs to insert "trouble and pain" programs into the barrier, and by this adding more energies to the astral plane, cf. the CSBs need the enclosure and the astral plane to be able to unfold their crystalline agenda. The crystalline technologies utilize the astral energies and from these generate the crystalline silicate matrix, the TEGs (strands) connected hereto etc. Thus in these days and ahead, they will do whatever it takes to generate more astral energy, affecting the humans linked emotionally and mentally to the astral barrier (the enclosure, the astral barrier, the astral plane are one and the same thing from three different levels; the enclosure was the blueprint, the barrier the result of this blueprint, the plane the result of the quarantine).

Or the other result could be, if the DE2D4 avians leave, making the DE1D3 a predominantly reptoid area:

B) The Sirian B-Reptoid Wars in our quadrant, which ends with wiping out all of the reptilian-reptoid races and by this impairing the LPU from a huge chunk of its gene pool. All genes are needed for the LPU to re-attach to the HM.

There are no solutions to this for the present, but naturally we – the councils – cannot prevent the DE2D4 from accessing this huge opportunity, but on the other side, leaving only the DE2D5 races here will pose new issues to be dealt with, albeit the DE1D3 has been for a long time under the "guardianship" of the DE2D5 races and will be that in the future as well, due to the NSEH and NOA coalition and their strong political take over taking place right now and in the years to come.

If the DE2D4 avian races agree to stay and instead link the sun and its gridworks to the DE1D3 this will create new issues too. The climate and space weather issue that arises from the entering sun is a whole other thing, since its presence affects the QFFs of our reality infusing it with more 4D energies.

The most important information in this for most of you is to avoid adding more astral energies to the barrier. That is the first thing to be learned and an important one. Obstacles in forms of humans and their behavior is one part of the "trouble and pain" programs, events, catastrophes etc involving humans are another.

For those of you who carry avian genetics this could be an opportunity to work with your avian genetics. Not as in linking up to the gridworks connected to the entering sun, but to sort of pull out the effect of it from our QFFs to sustain and heal some of the regressed genetics many of us hold.

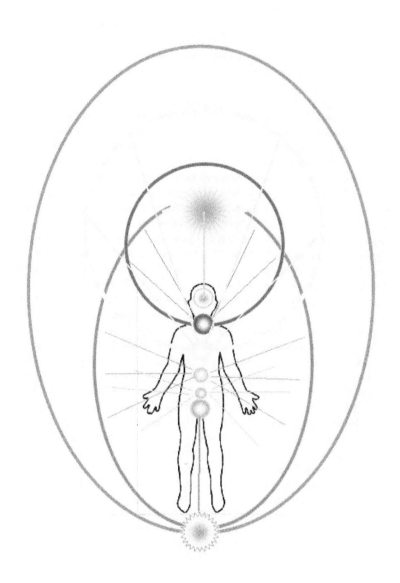

See All of My Work

I have a blog, where I share the information I get from the Councils etc: Rebuilding Earth on http://planetaryupdates.blogspot.dk/

I also have three video channels on YouTube. You find them by going into my website under Rebuilding Earth.

Join on Facebook, also to be found on the website.

And naturally my website with educations, all the tools you need in your personal progress and much more. Find it on: www.toveje.dk

We are facing a new future as the sun, the planet and the solar system reset around us. Only the "human world" remains to make the shift and humanity is the keyplayers in this. We need to prepare as a species to stand up to the other stellar races that are waiting in the wings to take over our home. Our tools are not technology but the energy and consciousness from the Soul level.

www.toveje.dk

CPSIA information can be obtained
at www.ICGtesting.com
Printed in the USA
BVHW09s0055121018
529911BV00001B/283/P